Fr. Ron was quite the priest, indeed! — Joyce F.

A rich treasure of reflections from colleagues, superiors, parishioners and family members compiled in an easy-to-read, hard to put down book. Gems of remembrances topped off by Fr Ron's own Christmas letter of 2016 (just a handful of months before his death) to his friends wherein his energy, imagination and resolve to continue on with the work of the Lord comes shining through! — Jon and Sue M.

Get the companion volume:

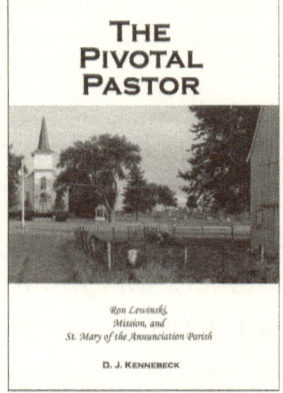

The Pivotal Pastor tells the story of how a nationally known priest (Ron Lewinski), a world-renowned architect (Dirk Lohan), and a farming community collaborated to build a new church on 33 acres of Illinois farmland at the turn of the millennium. It is a story about vision, leadership, teamwork, communication, change, and transition. During the 6-year project, the parish grew from 600 to 1,200 households, built a church to accommodate 900 (the old one held 200), and increased ministries from a handful to nearly three dozen. This $11 million project achieved what many thought was impossible. The story is historical non-fiction and includes content from materials that only the author had access to.

This is the most unique and detailed account of this parish's accomplishments that has been written. While it describes serious work, it is peppered with personal insights, anecdotes, and humor. It describes the experience of a particular pastor and parish, but the book is meant to help all Christian pastors recognize their ability to be pivotal within their own circumstances. The book is written by D.J. Kennebeck, editor of *Remembering Ron Lewinski*.

Visit www.emmaus-way.com/tpp

for information and to order. ISBN: 979-8-9866668-0-8 (Paperback)

Reader reactions to THE PIVOTAL PASTOR, by D. J. Kennebeck

I found this book to be engaging, well written, and a masterpiece homage to a wonderful pastor and the God Who drove his spirit! — Kathi B.

This is a very comprehensive book with extensive details. It's well written and flows with an engaging story. I'm finding it very interesting as I learn more about Fr. Ron and the process that unfolded during the building of the new church. I highly recommend it, especially for parishioners of St Mary of the Annunciation. Awesome book! --Tom W.

Every Deanery, every parish should have a copy and make pastors and parishioners aware of it when they are to embark on a building project. While reading, I experienced deja vu from my committee service when fundraising for our parish center. This book should serve as a 'blue print', helping supporters prepare for their service. — Joyce F.

Really enjoyed the book. It walks through the whole process, starting with a vision that developed and matured into a plan with parishioner inputs and then was brought to reality. The first-hand accounts and details on discussions gave insight on the process that created such a beautiful building. It helped me understand the development and appreciate the meaning behind the architectural choices. — John B.
`

The Pivotal Pastor is an amazing tribute to Fr. Ron Lewinski and what he accomplished in a small, relatively unknown, rural township in Illinois during his time as pastor at St. Mary's. Reading the details described in this book, I realized what a very special person we had. Truly he was hand picked by God to lead us through joys, sorrows, frustrations, and celebrations that culminated in the world class structure that is St. Mary of the Annunciation. He inspired the generosity and commitment of us parishioners who believed in his "dream" to make it happen. As an aside, this is a great primer for any church going through a building renewal either as a renovation or new build. Well done! — Jean B., parishioner

I had tears coming down my cheeks during much of the reading... so many people, so many hours, so much leadership by Ron Lewinski... not many could have accomplished this. — Anonymous parishioner

Excellent! Fr. Ron Lewinski was a classmate of mine and a beloved friend. The Pivotal Pastor *is a great tribute to him.* — Fr. F.

The author did a great job documenting Fr. Ron's vision and ministry principles relating to the building design, ministry philosophy, value of aesthetics and use of space throughout the entire building. Most importantly, he describes how Fr. Ron's vision in the construction of the church is used to glorify the name of God and uplift people in our community for generations to come. — Dan P.

Comments? Questions? Corrections?

Contact the author at
djkennebeck@emmaus-way.com

Additional copies of this
book are available from
www.emmaus-way.com/rr

For information about the parish of St. Mary of the Annunciation,
and additional information about Fr. Ron Lewinski,
see www.stmaryfc.org or write to them at
22333 W. Erhart Road, Mundelein IL 60060.
Inquire about a tour of the facilities.

Remembering Ron Lewinski

Remembrances of a Pastor, Priest, Man
by Clergy and Laity Who Knew Him

Edited by
D. J. Kennebeck
AUTHOR OF
THE PIVOTAL PASTOR

EMMAUS WAY LLC

FIRST EDITION

ISBN: 979-8-9866668-7-7 (Paperback)
ISBN: 979-8-9866668-2-2 (ebook)

Publisher's Cataloging-in-Publication data
Names: Kennebeck, David Joseph, editor.
Title: Remembering Ron Lewinski : remembrances of a pastor , priest , man / by clergy and laity who knew him; edited by D.J. Kennebeck.
Description: Includes bibliographical references and index. | Brooksville, FL: Emmaus Way LLC, 2023.
Identifiers: ISBN: 979-8-9866668-7-7 (paperback) | 979-8-9866668-2-2 (ebook)
Subjects: LCSH Lewinski, Ron. | Catholic Church--Clergy-- Mundelein (Ill.)--Biography. | Catholic Church--Clergy--Mundelein (Ill.)--Anecdotes. | BISAC BIOGRAPHY & AUTOBIOGRAPHY / Religious | RELIGION / Christianity / Catholic | RELIGION / Clergy | ARCHITECTURE / Buildings / Religious | HISTORY / United States / State & Local / Midwest (IA, IL, IN, KS, MI, MN, MO, ND, NE, OH, SD, WI)
Classification: LCC BX4705 .L49 K46 2023 | DDC 271/.5302/092--dc23

Book design by David J. Kennebeck. Assembled using Scrivener and other tools.
Front cover: leather-like background is from Vecteezy.com. The cross of gold tiles was arranged by Fr.. Ron Lewinski.
Photo of the cross courtesy of parishioner Darrell Harmon.
Back cover photo of Fr. Lewinski (circa 2017) is copyright Liturgy Training Publications, from their
video: https://www.youtube.com/watch?v=yZqrE0mpTz4. Used with permission.
Image of the Good Shepherd statue following dedication page is by D.J. Kennebeck.

Published by Emmaus Way LLC.
Printed in the United States of America.
www.emmaus-way.com

First Print Edition 2023
1 2 3 4 5 6 ..

In Memory of Rev. Ronald J. Lewinski:
a servant of the Cardinal and of the Church

Associate Pastor
Author
Board President
Brother
Classmate
Client
Co-Director
Consultant
Cousin
Dean
Director
Disciple
Dreamer
Father
Friend
Leader
Learner
Liturgist
Manager
Mentor
Pastor
Peer
Preacher
Priest
Son
Speaker
Stranger
Student
Teacher
Uncle
Visionary

*And with gratitude to those who have passed subsequent to
sharing their remembrances within these pages.*

The Good Shepherd

What I've observed after many years as a priest is that the experiences for which I am most profoundly grateful are nearly all experiences I didn't initiate. I didn't dream them up myself. A need I wasn't looking for came my way. I heard a call. And I responded as best I knew how. And the fruits of these experiences have been far beyond anything I could have predicted.

—Rev. Ronald J. Lewinski
From his acceptance speech in 2017
after receiving the "As Those Who Serve" award
from the University of St. Mary of the Lake,
where he was ordained 45 years earlier.

Introduction

This book evolved while I was researching and writing another book, "The Pivotal Pastor." In a way, this is a companion volume to that book.[1]

"The Pivotal Pastor" is my telling of Fr. Ron Lewinski's first of three six-year terms (1996-2002) as Pastor at St. Mary of the Annunciation parish near Mundelein, IL. During that time, Ron transformed the parish from a "little country parish" into an active faith community by leading the community in an $11 million project and constructing a new church—designed by the world-class architect, Dirk Lohan—that holds four times as many people as the old church (which was respectfully retained).

I was part of that experience and knew Fr. Ron Lewinski as a friend and pastor. But when beginning my inspired journey of writing about it, I felt a need to hear other perspectives about Ron. I collected most comments via interviews conducted over the phone or in person. Some people opted to submit written "content" instead.

As I was finishing "The Pivotal Pastor," five years later, I realized that only a small percentage of the material that I'd collected was actually included in that book. When I read through the unused content I decided it deserved to be shared. This book is the result.

Why bother publishing the "left over" material? I think, after reading these memoirs, that will no longer be a question for you. Meanwhile, I'll share some of my reasons.

First, in gratitude to the many people who generously shared their memories with the expectation that doing so would be fruitful.

Second, there is interesting and informative content that gives a fuller portrait of the man people knew as Fr. Lewinski, or "Ron."

Third, I believe Ron Lewinski was one of the few truly "authentic" people one encounters during their life. That doesn't mean everyone liked him, or that he was "better" than others. Rather, it means he was someone who found his purpose in life and pursued it consistently and with integrity. He didn't do it for recognition; he was humble (although he felt affirmed and enjoyed when other people acknowledged his work). He did not pursue material wealth, for surely he could have chosen other vocations in which to apply his

---

1. Paperback ISBN 979-8-9866668-0-8; www.emmaus-way.com/tpp

gifts "profitably" for that purpose. He did not seek power; otherwise, he could have chosen a path within the Church's hierarchy. Instead, I think he amplified his gifts and allowed himself to become a voice of the Spirit, drawing forth the God-given uniqueness within others and fostering its development and expression. He was a vehicle for fueling the flame of other's lives.

This book would not exist without the contributions of everyone identified in the list of Contributors. Because the content didn't begin as an intentional collection of memoirs, the "tone" of the material varies from one contributor to another. I regard that as a diversity to be enjoyed.

Contributors to these memoirs range from someone who had only a few hours of conversation with Fr. Ron to others who knew him for over sixty years. The descriptions of Fr. Ron include commonly recognized traits: humor, authenticity, love for liturgy, humility, vision, and leadership. There is recognition of the paradox that he was an introvert who actively socialized. He was an intellectual who wrestled with religious theologies as readily as he did with a young teen who would later become an award-winning wrestler in college. Ron enjoyed swimming in community pools and backyard lakes, and was adept at navigating the hierarchies of clergy in the local and national church.

The reader may wonder why I begin the book with a reflection from Fr. Ron about taking a retreat. Well, I regard these memoirs as something deserving more than just a "reading." In fact, I suggest the reader not approach this book with the intent of reading "normally": from beginning to end. Instead, I propose the reader approach it in "pieces," choosing to read "chapters" sequentially or randomly, but perhaps never more than a handful at a time. Or, in the case of the longer chapters, perhaps one chapter at a time.

Each contributor's content, in its own chapter, includes observations that I think warrant some degree of contemplation. The many people who have offered to share their perspective of Fr. Ron should be acknowledged for their generosity. Reading with intentional patience will respect the spirit of their contribution. There are commonalities to be recognized, but the differences should be equally valued. Furthermore, contributors share some insights that aren't solely about Ron Lewinski, just as this book isn't only about Ron Lewinski.

As I was assembling this collection I would often regard it as a treasure of sorts. According to the author of one biography of Winston Churchill, there were, at the time this biographer wrote his book, already 1,000 other Churchill biographies. How could there be so many books about one particular person, and why add another to the list? After assembling this collection of memoirs, I believe the answer is that there are as many perspectives of someone or something as there are viewers. Each perspective is a special gem of its own; a collection of gems is a treasure.

Certainly there is value derived from simply reading an individual memoir. But I would like to think that the reader, by applying thoughtful intent, will dig past the surface value of a memoir and come to recognize meaning. What is contained within the memoir —in the form of a paragraph, a sentence, or perhaps even a phase or just a word—that snags your attention? If you knew Ron Lewinski, what causes you to recognize a similarity to your own perspective, or presents a challenge that advocates for some change in your attitude? Spending time pondering these memoirs may help you recognize more of their value, just as time spent in contemplation during a retreat often produces lasting benefits that were not expected.

By the way, the contributors to this book are a fraction of those I initially approached while researching "The Pivotal Pastor." Many accepted my request to chat, some declined, many didn't respond. I feel obliged to apologize to anyone who might wish they had been included as a contributor. I hope you'll recognize that Fr. Ron's connections were many, and there are practical restraints on my time and effort.

It has been my privilege to assemble this collection. I hope you find these "memoirs" insightful, and sometimes even motivational. For those who knew Fr. Ron, be warned: some of this content may cause fond memories to surface. They did for me.

D.J. Kennebeck
2/15/23

About the content

I. The value "St. Mary's" is used to identify "St. Mary of the Annunciation" (formerly St. Mary at Fremont Center) parish.

II. There are other acronyms, abbreviations, and references to topics or concepts that the reader may not be familiar with. Rather than include explanatory footnotes that would disrupt the reading, I suggest the reader research whatever they need to. Having handy access to the Internet, or another comprehensive source, could prove useful.

III. Having said that, I have provided context for some phrases in a section called NOTES. They are organized according to the remembrance in which they appear. The reader may gain some benefit from reading the NOTES for a contributor prior to reading the contributor's remembrance.

IV. The "chapters" are the expressions of the contributors. There is no applied consistency of topic or structure.

V. The Concordance helps identify relationships by alphabetically listing topics and the contributors who mention them.

VI. Each remembrance is titled with the name of the contributor. Then comes a brief description of their *current* "position." If their relationship to Fr. Ron changed over time (e.g. since 2000) then their current title/role is given *first*, followed by their title/role at the time of Fr. Ron's first years at St. Mary's parish (1996-2000). This is followed by a brief "bio" (or "CV") in boldface. Last comes the contributor's comments.

VII. Page numbers, and an Index, are largely irrelevant so they have been intentionally omitted.

VIII. Contributors did not see other contributor's content prior to publication, but sometimes one contributor mentions another contributor by name. In that case, the *referenced* contributor's name is followed by an asterisk in brackets so the reader is aware there is also content from that contributor.

IX. The material on these pages originated with comments that people provided to me in verbal or written form. Because most people will say something differently than they would write it, I've edited the material for length and clarity while seeking to retain the intent of the speaker. (Prior to publication, contributors were offered the opportunity to review and edit their material, but not that of others.)

X. The 'expansion' or 'project' refers to the St. Mary of the Annunciation's successful effort to acquire land and build new facilities. It began in 1996 with Fr. Ron's arrival. The new church was dedicated in 2002. That historic story is told in *"The Pivotal Pastor."*

APRIL 14, 2000[2]
By Fr. Ron Lewinski
Pastor, St. Mary of the Annunciation Parish

I will be going on retreat this week to the Trappist Abbey in Gethsemani, KY. I've been going to Gethsemani for more than 30 years. It's the best place I've ever found to experience the silence and solitude that is so helpful in refreshing the soul.

So what does one do on a retreat like this? I find it's something like a melt down. When I first arrive I'm usually still feeling overloaded with all kinds of things that are on my mind about the parish. I carry a "to do" list with me in my head wherever I go. There's the building project, school issues, hurting families, troubled teens, wedding preparations, financial responsibilities, glaring needs I've seen and expectations I've heard in different ways. Someone said to me, "Have a good retreat and just forget about the parish." I don't think that's possible since my life is so intimately connected with the parish. But the silence and solitude of the abbey seem to have a soothing power to put all these concerns and more in perspective. What happens in the midst of the simplicity, quiet and prayerfulness of the place is a sorting out of issues, and a refocusing on the Lord who is at the center of all things. Even in the midst of doing church work, it's sad to say, but true, the centrality of Christ can be blurred by the issues and concerns of our own making. New energy and new insight flow from being anchored in the Lord.

I realize that is some ways a retreat like this is a luxury. (Thank God the church requires it of all priests or we might put it off). While it may be hard for busy parents and others to find the time for a retreat, the idea behind a retreat is worth going after. Maybe you can't spare five days right now. Can you take a weekend? A day? An afternoon? An hour a day? When we are constantly bombarded by so

---

2. Fr. Lewinski's comments were written two years to the day prior to the dedication of the new church at St. Mary of the Annunciation. Lewinski's reflections in this article were written just prior to Holy Week, a worship period that he revered. He seems to be suggesting that if one hasn't yet made time for a retreat during Lent, it is never too late — whether during Lent, or any other time. While he does not explicitly mention it, praying the Liturgy of the Hours — a practice the church requires of priests--is another means of taking time to acknowledge advice from scripture: "Pray without ceasing." (1 Thes 5:17) The Liturgy of the Hours is still available in print format. Readers who prefer digital (Kindle, Android, iPad, iPhone) can use the "IBreviary" app.

many things, it's easy to lose focus. What really matters in your life? Where is the passion? How much time and effort do you give to what is truly important to you? How does God fit into all that you do? If Jesus spent a week as a guest in your house, what advice would he give you at the end of his stay? If you died today and appeared before the Lord and he asked you: "What have you done with the gifts I gave you?" what would your answer be?

Where can one make a retreat? There are retreat houses one can go to, but there's also a bench in the forest preserve, a quiet room in the house or backyard patio, a lunch break taken quietly apart, etc. When you find your time and place, begin with a few words of scripture and let those words sink deep. Listen to a piece of music and let the sound and rhythm take you where it will. Or try keeping a journal. Find a picture or sacred image to focus your attention. Most important of all, just soak up the silence. Don't turn this retreat time into another "to do" that sets up yet one more burden to carry.

So important are these retreat moments for us all that I've really been thinking we have to provide that kind of quiet space right here at the parish. Our Eucharistic Chapel in the new church will be that kind of space, conducive to a self-made retreat. But even now, our church is open during the day - a quiet place to be apart. I sense there's an openness to the spiritual path I'm suggesting here, but I think we may also have to provide some spiritual guides to direct us on that path, to teach us a few steps that can point us in the right direction. We want to cultivate a stronger community life in the parish, but multiple parish activities are not the only answer. We need that retreat time, however you define it, that brings us back to the center - who is Christ. We need the strength that comes from the silence and solitude to engage more effectively in other activities.

NOTES

ARATA

~ "...The Wirtz's had land ..." — refers to Bill Wirtz and his family, owners of the Chicago Blackhawks when the parish sought land for expansion in 1997.

~ "...'Moms and Tots' and sister Gael ..." — Sr. Gael Gensler was Pastoral Associate during the expansion. Growing the ministries was one of her responsibilities, which she did with great success.

BAILEY

~ "...he had been leading RCIA..." — Lewinski was one of the "Fathers" of The Rite of Christian Initiation of Adults (RCIA), having begun a lifelong relationship with it when it was in its infancy, even before he was ordained.

~ "... Renew My Church ..." — A process in the Chicago Archdiocese that seeks to make disciples, build community, and inspire witness—in light of people's Baptism and Confirmation—working with the Holy Spirit. An earlier process, "Parish Transformation," engaged parishes in a facilitated self-examination of their community.

BARRETT

~ "...the right side looks and seems wider than the left side..." — The reason for this appearance is because the sanctuary space, a large square, is bisected by a nave that is on a slightly diagonal axis instead of running parallel to the side walls in the middle of the space. This is an intentional design feature and causes the exterior roof to appear "crooked" when in fact it is not.

~ "...it's all Fremont Center..." — Technically this is the township where the parish, previously called St. Mary at Fremont Center, is located although its mailing address (and commonly referenced location) is Mundelein, IL.

BEHM

~ "...doughnut-shaped base for the steeple..." — The church steeple was designed to be placed directly over the altar in the sanctuary, thus Lewinski's insistence on the correct location of the doughnut-hole. The steeple was originally intended to funnel light from the exterior down upon the altar; but architectural requirements thwarted the effect.

~ "...a church with all that glass..." — The 40-foot walls of the narthex, situated between the sanctuary and the pastoral center, are entirely glass. This was an initial concern until parishioners understood that the architect had done other major projects using glass including the Shedd Oceanarium and the Adler Planetarium in Chicago.

FR. GERARD BROCCOLO

~ "...the CCD office..." — Confraternity of Christian Doctrine. Related to Christian education, commonly using the Catechism. It is often used to refer to religious education in parochial schools and is also known as REP (Religious Education Program). The usage here refers to a precursor of what has become known as the Liturgy Office which exists to support the Bishop of the diocese (in this case, the Archbishop of Chicago) and his parishes.

~ "...Mundelein Seminary..." — The seminary Fr. Lewinski attended and later taught at, in Mundelein IL. The town's population grew from 21,000 in 1990 to 31,000 in 2000 and remains there in 2020. Also known as the University of St. Mary of the Lake (USML), the seminary is named after George Cardinal Mundelein. In 1926, it hosted the XXVIII International Eucharistic Congress which was attended by 800,000 people.

MSGR. JOHN CANARY

~ "...the architect and the historical connections with Mies van der Rohe..." — The architect of the new church at St. Mary's is Dirk Lohan, grandson of German-American architect Ludwig Mies van der Rohe (1886-1969) who is often associated with the phrases "less is more" and "God is in the details."

~ "...Frassati school..." — An elementary and middle school, Frassati Catholic Academy was founded to serve multiple parishes during Lewinski's third term at St. Mary's parish. Lewinski was a key leader in establishing the school. He became its first President.

SR. AGNES CUNNINGHAM

~ "...he came to appreciate his own baptism..." — Lewinski regularly celebrated both his birthday (February 15) and his date of Baptism (March 3). One of his nicknames was "Ron the Baptist."

CARDINAL BLASE JOSEPH CUPICH

~ "...Department of Parish Life and Formation..." — This department initiated the Archdiocesan-wide process "Renew My Church" (RMC) that succeeded "Parish Transformation" which had impacted over 200 parishes in the Archdiocese. Lewinski's work with the RCIA substantially contributed to both programs.

BISHOP FRANZ-PETER TEBARTZ-VAN ELST

~ "...saw the church illuminated..." — From the beginning, Lewinski's design for the church included an illuminated steeple representing a beacon "in an oasis." With the inclusion of the glass narthex, the building's illumination at night is even more striking.

~ "...so many people at his funeral..." — Fr. Lewinski's funeral on July 26, 2017 was presided over by Cardinal Cupich, several bishops, and over 120 ordained clergy (some from outside the Archdiocese and even outside the United States). The standing-room-only congregation overflowed from the sanctuary into the narthex.

FAHEY

~ "...he would have missed Merton..." — "Merton" refers to the monk Thomas Merton, an influential writer best known for his autobiographical account of conversion in 1948's "The Seven Storey Mountain." Merton resided at the Abbey of Gethsemani where Lewinski took annual retreats during his priesthood. Merton died in Bangkok in 1968, four years before Lewinski was ordained.

~ "...they could turn part of it into a golf course..." — A bit of irony in this story is that Mundelein Seminary, where Lewinski was ordained, boasts a golf course adjacent to the campus. The course occupies land that belonged to the Seminary. It was expanded to 18 holes in 1929 because Cardinal Mundelein's doctor told him he needed to walk more. Known as the Pine Meadow Golf Club, in 1986 it was named the Best New Public Course by Golf Magazine and has received numerous awards since, including one of America's top 25 Public Courses.

~ "...resided in the parish where he worked..." — Lewinski resided at different parishes over time, but sometimes worked elsewhere, such as the ODW in Chicago.

SR. GAEL GENSLER

~ "...after Mass at Diantha Hall ..." — Diantha Hall, named after a parishioner, is an expansion to the school—including a gym—that St. Mary's completed long before Lewinski's arrival. Soon after, he selected the gym for weekend services because it could hold twice as many people as the old church. This required parishioners to set up and tear down the folding chairs and wooden platforms each weekend, which they did for five years until the new church was dedicated in 2002.

HERTEL

~ "...in 2017 at St Theresa in Palatine..." — Lewinski resided at St. Theresa in a Chicago suburb while working at the Archdiocese in Chicago. He passed in the rectory at St. Theresa on July 19, 2017.

~ "...a box of gold tiles he wanted inlaid..."— "The Pivotal Pastor" shows Lewinski arranging these tiles. A photo of the cross appears on the cover of this book.

BISHOP GERALD KICANAS

~ "...something that could be valuable to other parishes..." — This theme can actually be traced back to Lewinski's childhood as an altar server (See Zygmunt's remembrances.) It manifests at the seminary, during his sabbatical in 1994-1995, his application of his learnings to the St. Mary's expansion, and later Archdiocesan programs. In short, a vibrant liturgy was Ron's life-long pursuit.

SR. ELAINE MARIE KLUGIEWICZ

~ "...one class for each grade at Pullman..." — Though born in Hammond, IN, Lewinski's family moved and he attended Assumption B.V.M. Elementary School in Chicago's South Side community known as Pullman.

~ "...you could see the reaction in him..." — Sr. Klugiewicz was probably the first to observe this lifelong trait of Lewinski's. Though humble and vocally self-critical, recognition by others provided Lewinski an inner satisfaction and motivation to achieve more.

LOHAN

~ "...I first visited the Farnsworth House..." — The Farnsworth House was designed and constructed by Ludwig Mies van der Rohe, Dirk Lohan's grandfather, after World War II. It is a 1,500 square-foot one-room weekend retreat in rural Plano, Illinois. The steel and glass house was commissioned by Edith Farnsworth, and is one of AIA Illinois' "25 must see" buildings in Illinois.

~ "...I went up to St. Mary parish and looked around..." — While it doesn't seem unusual for an architect to explore, the belief by the project team is that Dirk Lohan was the only architectural candidate to "walk the site" and show a special interest in the potential of the project.

~ "...the character of a big barn in terms of shape..." — Some parishioner's comments about an artist's rendering of the design was that it reminded them of a corn crib between two pig pens. The critics apparently didn't recognize the irony in their comment. The parish had asked the architect to retain the rural nature of the farming community.

~ "...hide it but make it audible..." — The 2,800+ pipes of the organ at St. Mary's are installed in a room-sized alcove above and behind the altar. A wall of vertical wooden slats hides the pipes, except for a cutout on the right side which exposes some of the largest ones. Thus the visual appearance is ornamental without being distracting. Furthermore, fabric installed behind the wood slats visually hides the pipes but allows the sound to penetrate into the sanctuary. Thus, it is hidden, but quite audible.

DEACON JOHN LUCAS

~ "...It is truly a reflection of who he was..." — This statement echoes one by Cardinal Cupich when, while presiding at Fr. Lewinski's Funeral Mass, he stated "to worship in this church is to be in the presence of Ron Lewinski."

LYMAN

~ "...The ceremonial doors..." — The story of these doors, which had been discarded from the plans until an act of Providence, is related in "The Pivotal Pastor."

MARKIEWICZ

~ "...that is what happened..." — The "Pastoral Statement of US Catholic Bishops on Persons with Disabilities" (rev. 1989) states: "Accessibility involves far more than physical alterations to parish buildings. Realistic provision must be made for Catholics with disabilities to participate fully in the Eucharist and other liturgical celebrations."

STOWE

~ "...program for people with special needs called SPRED..." — The Special Religious Development (SPRED) Program serves children and young adults with developmental disabilities such as Down syndrome, autism, and learning disabilities.

THOMPSON

~ "...Another book [by Merton] was about contemplation..." — Likely "The Springs of Contemplation" or perhaps "New Seeds of Contemplation."

FR. BOB TONELLI

~ "...not music that the older people adapted to..." — As an example, a 1993 survey at St. Mary's showed that nearly 80% of parishioners over the age of 65 preferred only organ music, compared to 50% of those between 55 and 65, and less than 25% of those under 25. During Lewinski's pastorship, instruments were expanded from organ and piano to include french horn, harp, violin, trombone, trumpet, tuba, guitar, flute, hand bells, and tambourine.

~ "...people don't understand: this is an American thing..." — in "The Pivotal Pastor," the chapter "A Campus Walk-through" describes Lewinski confronting this mis-perception.

~ "...Ron had asked if I had ever seen the Basilica of St. Clement..." — "Clement" also happens to be the name of Lewinski's father.

~ "...We needed an idea about how we could say farewell to the old church..." — St. John's parish was fortunate to convert their old church into a Parish Center. Soon after arriving at St. Mary's parish, Lewinski promised that the old church would not be grazed. He made this promise without knowing how the parish would be able to grow within the limited confines of the existing campus. He had faith they would find a way. The old church continues to be a house of worship on the parish campus.

SR. CORINE WALSH

~ "...Liturgy of the Hours..." — Another of the contributors mentioned that Fr. Ron would be the first to recommend that everyone pray the Liturgy of the Hours. It is available in book form as well as the app "iBreviary" for tablets and phones.

~ "...what he was doing and how he did it..." — This is a reference to the $11 million expansion project that Lewinski led during his first term at St. Mary parish. Over the course of six years, the number of households doubled, ministries quadrupled, and a new church was built that holds four times more than the old one.

WASHBURN

~ "...an abbey that really had an effect on the committee..." — This is St. Procopius Abbey in Lisle, IL. Early in the project, a team of parishioners accompanied Lewinski during visits to locations that could provide ideas and inspiration about what a future St. Mary's parish might look like.

~ "...the altar and an adjoining backdrop..." — see LOHAN, "hide it but make it audible."

JIM WOJCIK

~ "...the entire parish should go through the RCIA process..." — Although there is a "process," Lewinski's approach to RCIA was to enable someone to pursue it as inspired by the Holy Spirit rather than as a rigid curriculum with pre-defined beginning and ending points.

FR. PETER WOJCIK

~ "...somebody interrupting a wedding..." — See also Howard Fischer's "Vigil" comments.

ZAGULA

~ "...the "why" behind everything..." — These questions are addressed in "The Pivotal Pastor," as well as in a document at St. Mary's parish office which is used by docents for guided tours of the facility.

Characteristics

Academic	Generous	Literate	Serious
Aloof	Genuine	Liturgist	Servant
Amiable	Good	Loving	Sharing
Analytical	High-intensity	Mature	Shy
Articulate	High-strung	Mild-mannered	Smart
Bashful	Highly organized	Multifaceted	Soft-spoken
Blessed man	Honest	Open	Stoic
Brilliant	Hospitable	Open-minded	Successful
Capable	Humorous	Outgoing	Supportive
Caring	Humble	Outspoken	Sweet
Charismatic	Impactful	Passionate	Talented writer
Compassionate	Impressive	Pastoral	Teacher
Complex	Inclusive	Patient	Theologian
Conflict-adverse	Influential	Pensive	Thorough
Creative	Innovative	Personable	Thoughtful
Dedicated	Insightful	Philosophical	Trusting
Detail-oriented	Intelligent	Progressive	Unassuming
Devout	Intense	Quiet	Uptight
Dreamer	Introvert	Realistic	Visionary
Emotional	Intuitive	Reflective	Warm
Encouraging	Inviting	Relate-able	Well-grounded
Enthusiastic	Kind	Respected	Well-spoken
Faithful	Knowledgeable	Restrained	Wise
Focused	Leader	Reverent	Witty
Friendly	Learner	Self-critical	Wonderful
Fun	Listener	Sensitive	Workaholic

Remembrances

Mike & Kathleen Arata

Parishioners
School/Parish Ministry Members and Leaders

Mike and Kathleen Arata joined the parish in September 1996. They became committed to parish and school growth and prosperity.

We both grew up outside of Philadelphia. Where you lived determined your parish. So when we moved here we asked what parish was associated with us. They said you can go where you want. We chose St. Mary's.

Our first impression of Fr. Ron was that he was a very shy man.

We had a very close priest friend in the Archdiocese, and he became a kind of extended family. So when we came up, we chatted about St. Mary's. He knew Fr. Ron very well. Rule number one was that Fr. Ron was a liturgist. The most feared priests in the world were liturgists. The portrayal was that he was a by-the-book liturgist, and he knew the "script" better than anybody. So the portrayal of him as a strict liturgist contrasted with getting to know him as a soft person with a dry chuckle here and there. He was just a very quiet and loving man.

I think he was extremely thoughtful. He would remember things and ask you about them later—something about your family or something that happened to someone. That was very striking. We came to enjoy his sense of humor. He would say something very quietly where only you could hear it. That became funny because you were laughing, but nobody else had heard what he said. He was a master at being at a large event and making sure that he saw everyone, doing his due diligence, and then disappearing. I used to tell people he was like the amazing invisible man. He was there one minute and when you turned around he was gone.

He was the most serious of all the priests we have ever known. We had seven priests at the altar when we got married. We've been around a lot of priests in our lives. Relative to other priests, Ron impressed me most as the greatest theologian of them all.

One of the seven priests that were at the altar is a candidate for sainthood. Bill Atkinson—an Augustinian.[3] He was the first quadriplegic ever ordained as a priest. He is one of the most amazing stories you would ever want to read about and he was a very close friend of mine and taught me in high school. During our wedding, he was at the altar.

The Wirtz's had land that butted up to St. Mary's and it seemed to be a no-brainer to work with the parish [during the expansion]. But apparently, they weren't inclined. That made me anti-Blackhawks for the rest of my life.

After Ron left St. Mary's, he still visited the parish, of course. He said Mass one day and I remember him starting his homily. He thanked everyone for studiously sitting in the same pews. I had to laugh. I looked around—oh, yeah, this family sits here and that family sits there. I thought that was pretty funny.

There was a lot during the project that had to do with Fr. Ron as a leader. Think about the ministries increasing. One of them was the "Moms and Tots" and Sr. Gael Gensler [*] encouraging that particular ministry. That is how we got to know so many people with kids. Through the years, as our kids have gone to different schools, they still keep in touch with other families.

I don't take it for granted, because I don't think it happens everywhere.

---

3. http://www.fatherbillatkinson.com/

David & Jean Bailey

Retired
Former parishioners at St. Mary of the Annunciation, active in the RCIA, choir, and
    committees during the expansion

We came to the parish almost when Fr. Ron did. We had known Fr. Ron before he was assigned to St. Mary's because for years he had been leading RCIA for the whole diocese. I knew him through that. David converted when we were in Lake Zurich at St. Francis DeSales. He went through the RCIA program there. So we often ran into Fr. Ron because that was his thing at the time. He was still assigned to Holy Name Cathedral because it was part of the Archdiocese under Cardinal Bernardin. The woman that was assigned to David as his sponsor had been Jewish and she converted. She was from St. Marceline's [Schaumburg], where Ron was once assigned. So that's how I knew Fr. Ron long before he was assigned to St. Mary.

David converted around 1993-1994. Fr. Ron was not assigned to a parish when David went through the program. You would go to Holy Name Cathedral for the Mass and for the RCIA. I knew Ron from there and I liked him. He wasn't much a part of the service itself. But he set everything up and made sure everything was running smoothly. He was very nice. A lady named Terri was our introduction to Fr. Ron. She spoke very highly of him at the time. He was always an intellectual. He knew the rubrics. He knew backward and forward what was right and wrong. He knew Canon Law.

Ron was going around the world. I know he went to Germany for RCIA, because Germany was witnessing what many European countries were: that the younger people were not coming to church. It was basically the older people. They wanted to know how they could get new blood into the Church. How do we do this? Of course, RCIA was one of the ways to do it. I think Ron went to Thailand, Germany and other places. There are much fewer Catholics once you get outside of the United States. Catholic churches in a lot of places are suffering because young people are not attending.

He went on sabbatical for the purpose of visiting parishes across the country to see why they were successful. That blended in with parish renewal. But he also traveled because of RCIA; that's how people knew him.

We actually met with Fr. Keusal, then pastor, when we first came to the parish. We went to a meeting with Fr. Keusal which is how he learned that David was not Catholic. David had been raised Lutheran. They are one of the few Protestant religions that believe the Eucharist is actually the body and blood of Christ. They've always believed that it is the consecrated Christ.

So when David went to Mass he felt that was similar to how he'd been raised. He did not have a problem going up to receive communion. But Fr. Keusal did. He made a whole homily about that fact. David almost got up and walked out at that point. But I said just wait, we'll leave right after Communion. And we never set foot back in that church again. David said I will never go there anymore.

When Ron came to St. Mary's, it was quite a change for the parish. We stayed away until Fr. Ron came. Then we said now it is time to go back. We loved the church. It was very small. It was very intimate. We came from St. Francis DeSales and we helped build that church too. Ron was a multifaceted man. A pastor is not the parish. The people are the parish. Which was a big change for the parish when Ron arrived.

Ron was always very sweet. One of his concerns was retirement. It was a big thing for him. He would say, "I don't know what I'm going to do." I know he was thinking in the next year or so he wanted to get down on paper for posterity what was in his brain.

I knew that the parish renewal thing was a huge thing to him. That's what he had been given to do, to get that going. That was an acknowledgment that the Church needed some new blood: how are we going to do this if we are to continue.

I know he enjoyed working on Renew My Church and he did well with it.

Kathi (and Tony) Barrett

Retired parishioners of St. Mary of the Annunciation
Kathi is a Former Director of RCIA at the parish

Kathi and her husband Tony have long been parishioners at St. Mary's parish.

I first met Fr. Ron on his first Sunday here. It wasn't much of a conversation because I really hadn't been involved a lot at the parish; Mass and occasional small committee stuff and things with the school. Ron seemed uncomfortable with the typical after-Mass-meet-and-greet in front of our 'little' Church. I later understood his discomfort to come from his being a bit of an introvert until you got to know him and he got to know you.

When I think of Fr. Ron, I guess I think of shy, unassuming, and always in deep thought. Most often, he was thinking anywhere from three months to ten years down the road. He sometimes seemed cold or indifferent, but as I grew to know him, I realized he was not that at all. I think that was one of his biggest stumbling blocks at St. Mary: people often misinterpreted his demeanor.

As I came to understand him better, my respect for him grew by leaps and bounds and I learned to easily work with him. He didn't like to be singled out for praise or acknowledgment. Mostly he saw himself as the perennial servant, just doing his job and fulfilling his vocation. He often deferred praise to someone else or would humbly accept praise by saying, "Yes, but there's still more to be done."

I recall one of the first meetings we had in planning the new church. We were in our little church basement and had been called together in a sort of "anyone who can come, please do" mode. We were soon taken aback by the amount of work and thought that was going to be needed. About an hour or so into it, Roger Fisher [*] stood up and said something that I've both never forgotten and quickly applied internally every time I met with or encountered Fr. Ron. Our group that evening was a bit argumentative, scattered, and kind of pushing against the grain.

Roger stood up and said, "Come on, Folks, we need to get on board here. You have no idea what we have here in this priest. His credentials speak for themselves and his vision is far beyond anything we could ever have anticipated possible for our parish. Don't think for a moment that this priest is going to be with us for long. The

Archdiocese would be fools not to tap into his genius and use him on a larger scale, diocese-wide. So we have to move on this now and trust this man's mind and wisdom. He's a gift!"

Going forward, keeping what Roger Fisher said in my mind, I watched as Fr. Ron turned our parish upside down and gave it back to us. My respect, admiration, and compassion for him grew as I saw our parish come alive. I think I could even say at some point I went from admiration to "awe" of his vision and knowledge. Right up to his death, he was an astounding thinker and total priest.

Fr. Ron and I had our own go-rounds over the years but I learned so much from him and gained so much from his wisdom and vision that I came to respect him in a way that some of the nay-sayers never bothered to try. I appreciated he was certainly more educated than I, much more a visionary than I, and in matters of the Church and parish, he was so very much wiser and in-tune with the issues, both current and future. We didn't always agree, but I quickly came to acknowledge that his suggestions reflected a broader perspective and a more futuristic and practical approach than mine. He quite simply projected greater wisdom than I, and I soon accepted and relied on it.

The United States Conference of Catholic Bishops (USCCB) wrote: "Built of Living Stones" (BLS) based on, and expanded from, Vatican II documents. It was approved by the Vatican and published in 2000. The BLS grew out of "Sacrosanctum Concilium" and its decrees on the dedication of a church; and on "Ordo dedicationis ecclesiae et altaris," dated 1977; and also the chapter on sacred art and furnishings.

Because it was developed by the USCCB and not the Vatican, they left it to the individual U.S. Bishops to enforce as much or as little within their individual jurisdictions provided their jurisdictions at the very least adhered to the Vatican II guidelines. Because of this rather loose enforcement of this document, you find in the U.S. some dioceses where it's gloriously evident that they took BLS very seriously and then other dioceses half-enforced it or not at all. You'd really need to know the document to be able to tell in a church how much or how little was applied. Yet all churches had to at least adhere to the Vatican II decree.

One of the main points of BLS is that if you're building a new church, you have to make a space where all the sacraments can be celebrated "largely." That was the basis for how Fr. Ron envisioned our new church, i.e., where to put the font so it is liturgically correct, where you position everything in the church so that it can accommodate, for instance, the Triduum, or a wedding, or confirmation, or all kinds of baptisms, infant, adult, conditional.

It was no coincidence Fr. Ron used both Vatican II and BLS when forming the concepts for St. Mary's. I look at our church and I say, "That's the BLS document." Ron got it right, even to the point in the BLS document that states whenever possible, anything in the church should be made by human hands. So I'm always amazed when I see all the things that actually were not manufactured but hand-made. The statues, the candle-holders, the stations of the cross, the altar, the ambo, the font, and the tapestries, for instance, are completely or largely made by individual people. I am amazed how our church is a living testament to the document.

The biggest surprise about the building, for me, was how much attention to detail Fr. Ron spent in adapting BLS to the character of our landscape and the character and history of our parish. When it was all put together, I just marveled at how every nook and cranny reflected his deep thought and execution of reason and purpose.

Ron wrote several books on the RCIA. The foundational vision for RCIA as designed in Vatican II, of course, remained the same and his writings always reflected that same foundation, but he offered it through the sacraments and how they should interweave methodically throughout a Candidate's formation. For example, when a Candidate has been previously baptized, how that baptism connects them to their desire to be confirmed in the Catholic Church and receive the Eucharist. His writings opened up the Catechist's eyes to see RCIA formation through the grace and power of the sacraments and the authority of the Holy Spirit.

In another book, he gave the parameters from the Vatican II document on the RCIA, and he showed how a year-round RCIA process correctly adapts to that vision. That's what we've used for twenty years at St. Mary. Many parishes adhere to a process that is basically based on a school year model where a Candidate can only begin around September or October. Then there's a certain lesson taught each week, and the Candidate moves toward Baptism, Confirmation, and First Eucharist during the Easter Vigil celebration. This model lacks submission to and acknowledgment of the will and movement of the Holy Spirit. It seems to deny that we individually arrive at our faith as the Spirit moves within us.

The problem, which he's written about so much, is that kind of structure takes out of the rite the aim of the rite. Fr. Ron recognized that many pastors would prefer a great number of Candidates being received into the Church at the same time during the Easter Vigil as opposed to receiving them when their Holy Spirit-driven individual formation is complete. Fr. Ron's vision and understanding of the rite was that the Holy Spirit sent Candidates to us at different times throughout the year so that the entire process would flow throughout the entire Liturgical year through a distinct combination of Scripture and discipleship. Along with regular sessions based on Scripture, the Candidates moved throughout the parish and throughout the community doing outreach like PADS [currently meaning "Providing Advocacy, Dignity, and Shelter"], serving at fundraising dinners and events, helping at our sharing parish soup kitchens, visiting the homebound, working with the Mass ushers and Sacristans, helping clean the Church, attending the Chrism Mass, doing food collection and distribution for Catholic Charities and the list goes on.

In short, just reaching out to our brothers in the spirit and heart of discipleship through the eyes of the sacraments and beatitudes to develop the heart of a true Catholic Christian. The mandates of the rite as written in Vatican II, and Fr. Ron's subsequent parish development of it was ultimately smoother and seemed less stressful than the school-year model. We brought them into the Church and set them on their way according to how they were spirit-driven. Some people took three months; some people took three years. And the point of it is Ron's quote, "We are not forming them for here. We are forming them for out there. We are forming them to go into the world and preach the gospel by who they are."

That theme always went through all of his books and his writing. One particular book, "What It Means to be a Sponsor," is probably the most definitive of his writings about what we are supposed to do with our candidates and catechumens. We're forming them according to our example for the world at large, not to be our best friend and go with us to Mass on Sunday. We're forming them for something larger than the parish, and discipleship is the baseline of all of it.

When I was in RCIA, I would take all the candidates and do a tour of the church. What I did was a liturgical tour of the church based on Fr. Ron's deep liturgical vision of it. He was a liturgical master. He understood the documents from Vatican II, especially BLS, so that the structure of the Church became and was truly an integral part of the liturgy. As one enters other churches, you often see statues and all the things that are supposed to be there. But you don't feel the liturgy exactly the same as you might within the walls of St. Mary. Everything is placed and intended as part of the liturgy. That, to me, is an astounding realization!

I look at how our space enhances every liturgy that would ever occur there. Thought and process is in every bit of it. For instance, one night I had an RCIA session and, as usual, I was the last to leave. I would go into the church by myself for a little while. This particular time I was sitting up front praying and listening to the baptismal font flowing behind me, looking at the vigil lights, and just kind of settling down after my RCIA session. When I got up and turned around, I was shocked to see Fr. Ron at the back of the church, just sitting there. He must've come in after me and I didn't hear him.

I said "Father. I didn't realize you were back there." He said he liked to come into the church and just sit there for a while.

"There's something I bet not many people have noticed," he said. "Come and stand at the baptismal font and look toward the front of the church. The ceiling in particular." So I did.

He said, "It seems uneven as the right side looks and seems wider than the left side."

"Yes," I replied, "I have noticed that."

He said, "Now let me take you up to the first step at the altar and we'll turn around and look at the back."

So we did that, and I said, "Now it looks like the other side is bigger; just the opposite."

"And what do you see above the doors there, the three epiphanies?" he asked, and then continued, "What does that remind you of?" Before I could answer he said, "When you came in it was one way, and when you left it was another way. Now, look at the tapestries."

So I studied them and said, "Oh my gosh, one tapestry is the Magi. They didn't go back to their homeland the same way they had come."

Then he said, "Now think of something else: when we bring up the gifts, what are they?"

I said, "They are wine and bread."

"What happens then?" he asked.

I responded, "They change into the body and blood of Christ."

"Yes," he said. "Think about this: nothing is as it seems. It is still bread and wine but it is the body and blood of Christ."

He said, "When you have come to Christ, you can't go back the same; you are changed, different. So the church, the walls, and the tapestries are about entering into the worship space with our earthly thoughts attitudes, and impressions. Then we come forward to receive the body and blood of Christ. When we turn and go back, we are not the same. We cannot come to Christ and go back the same. We are changed."

So whenever I did the church tours with my candidates, I did it "liturgically" —it was more meaningful to them, and it made sense about how everything was related. It became liturgical.

In the planning stages, I think we lost people when Fr. Ron announced we were having an immersion font. One man said, "I wouldn't go down in that thing." Then I said, "You don't have to, you're already baptized." He said, "I'm talking about other people." Initially, the immersion font was a big no-no for some during the planning sessions. I pointed out to as many folks as I could that Vatican II mandated we get back to our roots and methodologies, as with St. John the Baptist. After the Church was built and our first Baptisms were performed, people came to not only accept it but often brag about Baptisms at St. Mary.

Ron was humble to a fault. I would never find out from him when he'd written a new book. Do you know how I'd find out? When we'd receive the brochure from LTP, Liturgy Training Publications, Fr. Lewinski's publisher. I'd be going through it and see something by Ron Lewinski and I'd ask "What's this, when did he write this?" He'd never tell me in advance.

I still marvel each time I go to church and I never tire of looking around and seeing why something or another is the way it is. It's all Liturgical, it's all Fremont Center, it's all St. Mary.

Thank you, Fr. Ron Lewinski and thank you, God, for Ron's time with us.

Ken Behm

Parishioner, member of a founding family
Chair of the Land, Water and Septic committee

Ken and his wife Judy are longtime parishioners. Ken's ancestors were among the founders of the parish. His sister, Ann Steffenhagen, served as co-chair on the Capital Campaign committee.

I met Fr. Ron formally at the first meeting that I attended. It became pretty obvious that he was sent out here to expand the parish. I think that was his main purpose for being here. He had it in his head that we were going to get this church built. For five years, the Archdiocese had been wanting to expand the parish. Saddlebrook [a nearby retirement community], in a few years, brought 500 parishioners to St. Mary's. The only ministries I recall back then are the altar rosary society, the women's club, and a group that took care of the vestments and altar cloths and things.

At the first formal meeting, Fr. Ron set up dinner appointments at various houses, having between twelve and twenty people. Al Hertel had been taking care of the plumbing at the parish and Fr. Ron got with him pretty quickly. Ron did enough of his homework that he knew Al and I were good friends. He said, I know you were on the committee for the all-purpose room at St. Mary's school. So he made a dinner appointment at the Hertels. They invited Judy and me along with a couple of other couples. Fr. Ron had said he'd get the food, but Al said, no, we will take care of that.

I had formed two opinions of Fr. Ron. As a priest, he was a very priestly man, no monkeyshines, all business when it came to saying Mass or doing anything "religious." I came to understand that he was not a politician—he was direct. There were some people who took a tremendous liking to him, and other people, for lack of a better term, somewhat despised him. When he came to meetings, he was highly organized and didn't make idle talk. They sent him here to get this parish moving.

I know the doughnut-shaped base for the steeple was in the wrong place at one point and they had to move it eight feet. That's one thing Fr. Ron wouldn't give in. They said, well we can give you $100,000 credit if we can just leave it. He said no; it has to be over the altar. They said well we can move the altar. Ron refused.

There were a lot of questions about why would you build a church with all that glass, but now people think that's pretty nice. I remember the subject coming up in a lot of meetings about how we are going to be in that narthex with the sun coming in. Dirk Lohan [*] said, no we can use fritted glass. Somebody said it looks like a farm shed. He said that's exactly the purpose: people said they wanted it to be country-like—that's a country shed. In our narthex, the sun gets bright, but it never gets blinding. When all was said and done, I was very pleased with it.

From a priestly standpoint, Ron always had my respect. He was very holy, and if you had a question, he was more than willing to give an answer. I don't mean this to be derogatory, but he seemed to have a standoffish attitude. That used to bug a lot of people.

I respected Fr. Ron as a priest. He took care of the parish.

Fr. Britto Berchmans

Retired pastor of St. Paul of the Cross in Park Ridge, IL
Professor of Mass Communications at the Salesian Pontifical University in Rome

Fr. Berchmans is originally from India. Fr. Lewinski introduced him to St. Mary's parish. He has a Ph.D. in Communications from the University of Illinois, as well as degrees from other institutions: an Associate Degree in Western Philosophy; a Bachelor's and Master's in Physics; a Bachelor's in Theology; a Master's in Journalism; and a Master's in Systematic Theology (the last two from Marquette University in Milwaukee).

I was scheduled to teach a summer course at Marquette University in the summer of 1997. I was looking for a parish close to the Wisconsin border where I could stay and minister. Bishop Kicanas [*] suggested I stay at St Mary of the Annunciation. That's when I met Ron Lewinski.

My first impression of Ron was that he was serious but friendly. He invited me to stay with him in his condo. As I got to know him, I realized he was very personable and that he had a great sense of humor. I found him easy to talk to and work with.

Over time, we grew closer, and I began to consider him to be a mentor to me. In all the years I've ministered in Chicago, I turned to Ron when I needed some counsel. He was always there to help.

Ron was the ultimate professional. He was very organized and thoughtful. Ron was well-read and knowledgeable. He was an expert especially in the liturgy. Because of his many talents, the Archdiocese recruited him to lead its efforts to strengthen our parishes.

He was not the usual, serious-faced, average priest. He knew how to have fun and yet be focused on what he was supposed to do. For people who didn't know him, he appeared to be a little distant. Once you got to know him, you found out how friendly he was.

Ron was a firm believer in Vatican II, especially when it came to the liturgy. People invited him to do presentations on the subject in several parts of the world, including Malaysia and Australia.

He accomplished much in his life—not only by what he did for St Mary but also for the Church in general. He was certainly a great pastor. Building the new church was an achievement.

Ron is the one who asked me at the end of my stay with him in 1997, "Britto, would you ever consider coming to Chicago as a diocesan priest?" That question started the entire process. He was the one who encouraged me to come and arranged for me to meet with

Bishop Kicanas in the Spring of 1998. The bishop, in turn, introduced me to Cardinal George. Without Ron, I wouldn't have come to Chicago. I am deeply grateful to him. Even during my twenty-two years as an active priest of Chicago, he kept in touch with me and checked on me at priest's meetings. When I had questions, I went to him for advice.

His sense of the Church is something we should all emulate. He prepared his homilies carefully and took his role in the liturgy very seriously.

I wish more of us priests would take our preaching that seriously.

Fr. Gerard Broccolo

Emeritus Priest of the Archdiocese of Chicago
Pioneer of the Office for Divine Worship in the Archdiocese of Chicago

Fr. Broccolo has been a priest of the Archdiocese of Chicago serving in many roles.

In the early 1970s, Fr. Ted Stone was at what they called the CCD office. There was no "liturgy office." But Ted was very much into the liturgy in the aftermath of Vatican II. He, with the help of a lay couple—Tom and Mary Dore—was a pioneer in a lot of the early steps in liturgy reform and renewal after Vatican II for the Archdiocese of Chicago.

About that time, I had gotten my degree in liturgy and was returning to the diocese. We got started and two things happened. First, Ted Stone left the active ministry. Second, Tom Dore died.

Our auxiliary Bishop at the time and I started an Office for Divine Worship (ODW). We hired Fr. Dan Coughlin as the first Director. I was working with LTP. Unofficially, LTP was the publication arm of the ODW. I was called a consultant, and with Fr. Dan, we ran those two things together. That was around 1970 to 1972. Then it was decided we needed to expand. Shortly thereafter, I was moving on to other things. I had been teaching at Mundelein Seminary. The decision was made to bring in Gabe Huck [*] to head Liturgy Training Publications.

Dan Coughlin was getting ready to move on from the ODW in the mid to late 1970s, and he decided that one of the people he would hire at ODW was Ron Lewinski. So Dan hired Ron. In fact, Ron became Dan's protégé.

I was also in the process of moving on when Ron came on. So I wasn't involved with Ron in a lot of those early years of his work at ODW.

Angela Bujan

Spiritual Director, Speaker, Life Coach, and Founder of HELP Professional Services LLC
Former Parishioner, Coordinator of Women's Commission, Ministry Volunteer

Angela and her husband, Elliott, joined St. Mary's in 2002, shortly after the dedication of the new church. They have three children: Grace, Nicolas, and Gianna. Angela and her family were actively involved in many ministries, until they moved their family to La Crosse, Wisconsin in the middle of 2017. They still consider St. Mary's as part of their extended faith family.

One of the many positive things that came out of Fr. Ron being at St. Mary's was offering a Healing Mass for people who had lost children. My husband and I lost our first child, Nathan, and experienced very sacred moments in the midst of our grief. Although fairly new to the parish at the time, Elliott and I decided to coordinate a Healing Mass for others in our community dealing with loss. Fr. Ron was very supportive of our initiative and what we were trying to do because it hadn't been done before. We invited Fr. Ron and one of the deacons over to our house to discuss the plans and work out some of the details. That was one of the first times he was in our home.

He also worked with our son Nicolas, who was in the Boy Scouts. When our son got his religious medals, we met in Ron's office a few times to review what Nicolas had done and talk with him about the meaning and application. It was very clear, from a mentorship perspective, particularly with young people, that Ron would go the extra mile to encourage growth and learning in the next generation.

In terms of his personality, I would say Ron was a little shy, had a good "dry" sense of humor, and was very humble. One example that comes to mind is when we organized dinners for married couples in the parish. I remember him serving wine and taking pictures. I thought that was a wonderful example of servant leadership.

In terms of his strengths, he certainly was a visionary, a leader, and a talented writer. He had great respect for symbols and meaning, especially in the sacramentals, and often spoke with passion about the sacraments—in particular the sacrament of Baptism. I also had the privilege of co-writing a pilgrimage guide with him for the parish trip to the Holy Land, intended especially for those in the parish who could not physically travel. We developed a guide to accompany those who were in the Holy Land, as well as those staying at home.

Through scripture, guided prayers, and reflections, we could travel together as a parish. I also remember him telling me about the lights in the building. He pointed out architectural nuances that were very intentional, similar to some of the great cathedrals. The effort and intentionality put into the symbols were very evident.

In terms of his weaknesses, it is hard for me to comment. Some parishioners may have had concerns about his pastoral style. For example, people approaching him about family issues, perhaps Fr. Ron may not have always been the right person to sit down with one-on-one. We all have different gifts though, and it is not realistic to expect that someone will do everything well.

Fr. Ron clearly left an impression on many people. I continue to think about him often. Even in La Crosse, I ran into someone shortly after Ron's death who acknowledged our loss as a parish when they heard where I used to live. They said you must all be grieving.

Fr. Ron's notoriety is expansive. People think very dearly of him. I remember the last time we spoke after Mass, he said, "Pray for me." I have, and I continue to this day.

Msgr. John Canary

Friend of and brother priest with Lewinski since his ordination

Msgr. Canary was ordained a priest for the Archdiocese of Chicago in 1969. He was assigned to the College Seminary to teach Theology in 1972; in 1975, assigned to Mundelein Seminary; in 1995, named Rector of Mundelein Seminary; in 2006, named Vicar General of the Archdiocese of Chicago; and he was named the Director of the Joseph and Mary Retreat House in Mundelein in 2015.

I'm three years older than Ron. I was a deacon at St. Frances (Ron's first parish), then ordained a priest. The pastor at that parish, Msgr. Joe Howard, really kind of built a family spirit. When I was ordained priest I was assigned to a different parish, but he was always inviting people back. I knew the deacons who followed me very well so I maintained contact.

After I had been active on the south side for three years, I came back to St. Frances of Rome on Sunday for seventeen years. That's how I got to know Ron. He was in the seminary the same time I was so when I was a deacon he was only in first theology. He went two years to a college seminary in Niles, Illinois, and then, the last two years he actually came onto the campus at Mundelein and finished with a concentration in philosophy. So he was actually on the campus for six years: two of which were the last two years of college and then four years of theology. Then he was the Associate Pastor at St. Frances, a newly ordained priest, and I was coming to help on weekends. That's how I got to know him.

Ron probably would not have learned the 'old' way of doing things in the seminary, although he would have experienced it as a young boy. The changes began in the college seminary in 1961, and even though the liturgies were still primarily in Latin, there were certain parts of the liturgy that were in English. Then about '63 all the introductory rites, the readings, they were all in English. The "Sacrosanctum Concillium" document came out around '65.

The Council ended in 1965, so while Ron was in the seminary, all the results of the Council were taking effect. Easter of 1970 in the U.S. is when they changed the liturgy from Latin to English, so Ron was coming into the priesthood not only with all those changes but also with the document on the sacred liturgy. It just opened up for people a whole different experience of the liturgy.

At the seminary Ron would have been exposed to the high liturgies which were still in Latin. They also prayed the Liturgy of the Hours and that was in Latin; but that began to change in 1965, so he probably would not have experienced that. In 1966, Fr. Gorman [*] was appointed as the new Rector at the seminary and he really began to change the structures and the approaches to things.

Ron got very involved in the liturgy at St. Frances of Rome. There was a need for a lot of education of the parishioners and, for some priests, very much so. But at the parish level, he really created quite an extensive liturgy committee. I think part of his gift all the way along—even at St. Mary's—was that he not only educated people, but he put them into situations and structures that formed them. More and more they took responsibility as they were learning about the liturgy.

For Ron, the liturgy was a piece of the work of the Church—his ecclesiology—and as people became very excited as they began to understand more and more about how the liturgy is a source of life for the Church's mission.

A couple of differences between St. Frances and St. Mary parishes: the people at that time in Cicero were hard-working blue-collar folks. Many of them had finished high school. Very few had actually gone to college. So their interest in education was somewhat limited. That did not phase Ron at all. He gathered people, and he got them excited to read and to go to seminars to expand their own appreciation of our faith and their work. So that grew and became very strong over the years in terms of the vitality of that parish.

He had that capacity to bring people along. I saw that because I was there every Sunday. He was a newly ordained priest, so he had several questions like "Why do we do this, or how do we do this? How do we change this?" We'd bounce things off each other. To see his talent, his interests, his energies—it was pretty impressive for a young priest.

I think there were two great influences for him. One was Sr. Elaine Marie Klugiewicz [*]. I remember Ron talking about why he had such devotion to her: as a child, he really felt her belief in him. That gave him personal confidence. I think he certainly never forgot that; but he traced a lot of his determination and personal confidence to her. The other woman is Sr. Agnes Cunningham [*]. As an instructor at the seminary, her area of interest was Patrology: the study of the early Church writers, both men and women. She not only encouraged Ron's interest in them, but she pushed him. She also helped him to focus more on the roots of RCIA. So she was truly a great intellectual influence on him.

At the time, the old approach of sacramental theology was just focused on the "right way" of doing the ritual. Because of Vatican II, the seminary got beyond the ritual into the history and meaning of the sacraments, and why Baptism and the Eucharist were so important. Ron was in the middle of learning about that.

As pastor at St. Mary's, Ron wanted the parishioners to be deeply involved in the planning so that they'd grow in their own understanding that this was not just a building. This was about life together in faith and the different aspects of that. That gathering area —the narthex—at St. Mary's is a beautiful area. There's a whole theology that's connected with that.

I had several conversations with Ron as he was working on the expansion. He was very concerned that parishioners be involved. It was a formative experience for the parishioners. He knew it was one of those rare times when you actually had an opportunity to not just build a church, but to build Church and engage people. He was very excited when they selected the architect and the historical connections with Mies van der Rohe. His vision of what he was doing there was not simply building a building, but revitalizing the parish.

I lived with Cardinal George for eight years. I heard him several times talk about St. Mary's in glowing terms. At a certain point, Holy Name Cathedral in Chicago had some structural difficulties and he began talking about whether he would build a modern structure or a traditional structure. During that conversation, he did reference St. Mary's. He went out to Los Angeles when they dedicated their new cathedral. He came back and said there were two churches that he thought made an effort at having a modern design that was truly liturgical in all of its aspects. The Cathedral in Los Angeles, he said, almost made it. He said St. Mary's did make it. His perception, from my perspective, was very positive about St. Mary. I never heard any critique of St. Mary's from him.

Many of the activities that Fr. Ron was involved with—building a church, and Frassati Academy [Wauconda] —were all guided by deeper theological convictions. He wanted people to get excited about those things and not just the projects.

Ron was an outstanding priest, and Cardinal Cupich [*] recognized that right away.

Diane Ciesielski

Fr. Ron Lewinski's sister

When Ron visited us, we didn't ask questions about "work." And often when he was here, he spent most of his time writing, or his phone kept ringing. One time I said, "I thought you came here to get away and they're still calling you." He said, "Well, yes, that's the way it goes."

Ron did like to read. All the time. He came here with what I would call a suitcase of books. If I wanted some information for work, he would look up something for me.

A lot of people knew Ron. I remember Bishop Darcy, rest his soul. I worked at St. Joseph Church in Roanoke for thirty-two years. I worked for three different priests and the bishop would come for different occasions, and every time I was there he would say. "And you are…?" I would answer that I'm the secretary. We would go downtown and have a meeting, "And you are…?" He couldn't remember who I was, which I can understand.

Well then, we had some event like Confirmation or dinner, and Father said this is our secretary, Diane Ciesielski. The bishop asks "How long have you been here?" And Father says, "Well, maybe you know her brother, Fr. Ron Lewinski." So, the bishop says "Oh yes. Office for Divine Worship, RCIA…" He starts rattling off all the stuff that Ron was involved in and here I had met him over and over, but he couldn't remember me. After that, I was known as "Ron's sister." I just thought that was hilarious. One time I called Ron's office and the secretary asked who was calling, and I said this is his sister Diane. So he gets on the phone and says, "Hello Sister Diane, I didn't know that you had made your final vows." So after that I just said "Diane" and they knew who was calling.

Before the dedication Mass with the Cardinal, Ron called me and told me that one tapestry had not arrived and he was all upset. I said Ron, don't worry about it. No one knows what's supposed to be up there. He said, oh, I guess you're right.

When the smoke alarm went off during the dedication, I looked at him sitting in the Presider's chair and I could tell that he was hoping the floor would open up and swallow him. My daughter-in-law said I hope the sprinkler system doesn't go off. I loved when the

Cardinal got up and said Fr. Ron did a good job with this church—the smoke alarm works well. I felt so sorry for Ron.

The first time I met Sr. Gael Gensler [*] she took me aside and said, "Diane, if Ron ever wants to come to your house, you let him. He needs to get away." I said, "Sister, he is welcome to come anytime and stay as long as he wants." She replied, "Good, because he needs to get away from things." But when he would come here, what would he do? Writing or on the phone.

When we lived in Calumet City, we lived with grandparents. Then we went to West Pullman and lived with other grandparents. When we lived in Calumet City, my grandparents lived on Pulaski Road and my girlfriend lived across the street through a field. I said, "Mom, can I go to Maryann's house?" She would say yes, but you have to take Ronnie—he was only three years old, so I had to take him. Then one day I asked can I go to Maryann's house, and she said sure, Ronnie is going to stay home with me today. So I went out the front door, down the steps, and across the street, and I hear screeching tires. I turn around and there's Ronnie standing in front of a bus, about a foot away. He wasn't scared. He just ran after me asking, can I still go with you? When I got home later, my mother was furious at me. I said, "But mom you told me I could go by myself." And when my dad came home, well...

Ron was a "priest" even when he was a kid. When Rich and I got married, Ron was twelve years old, and he was an altar server. When I moved out, my bedroom became the chapel, and my dad built in a Presider's chair. I never actually saw Ron play priest, but obviously he did because why else would you want all that? When he was in eighth grade, he would go to the rectory and be there so the priests could take a break and Ron would answer the phone and the door. We didn't live that far from the church. He could walk there.

After eighth grade, he went to Quigley preparatory seminary so he wasn't around the house. From there, he went to Mundelein Seminary. We moved to Virginia, so we really lost touch for those four years. He would come for vacation because he liked to be with our kids.

He liked to roller skate. He used to roller skate on the streets—you know, that was the thing back then. Those were the skates that you would screw onto your shoes. Ron played racquetball, but once he busted his ankle. When we played darts, one would hit the ceiling, another would hit the floor. I had him as a partner, but we still won.

We have a neighbor, Chris Needler [*], and he'll come here or we'll go there. He wanted to meet "Fr. Ron." I promised to introduce them the next time we walked by his house. Usually, after dinner, Ron would like to walk. So Chris was out there and I said to Ron, I want you to meet my neighbor—he wants to talk with you. I introduced him and we sat out there until dark. Chris was shooting questions at Ron. The next day when I went over there, Chris said Ron was the smartest man he ever talked to. He asked Ron questions that for years nobody could answer, about several things. He liked him from that day on, and he would ask when is your brother coming to visit again?

I had just talked to him about a week before he passed. He said he had been overseas and he thought he picked up a bug. Well, I said, you better get to the doctor and find out what that is. A week later he died.

When I was at his funeral I admonished him. He was supposed to be at our funeral, we weren't supposed to attend his.

Sr. Agnes Cunningham

Retired
Former instructor at Mundelein Seminary and lifelong friend of Fr. Ron

Sister Agnes Cunningham was born on May 26, 1923, in Middlesborough, Yorkshire, England. She is an American patristic theology educator and author, ATS grantee, 1980, Lilly grantee, 1991. Member American Theological Society, Catholic Theological Society of America (president 1977-1978), International Association Patristic Scholars. She earned a Bachelor of Science from St. Louis University in 1954, a Master of Arts at Marquette University in 1963, a Licentiate of Sacred Theology from Facultés Catholiques in Lyon, France, in 1964, and an STD from Facultés Catholiques in 1968.

I started teaching at Mundelein Seminary in 1967. I taught for twenty-five years full-time and then another ten years part-time. As I look back over the twenty-five years, Ron Lewinski was one of the few that really seemed to understand what I hoped to give the students, to have them know how important the Fathers of the Church are.

Ron took to the Fathers of the Church like a fish to water. He was one of the students who encouraged me to ask the Dean's approval to split one general Patrology course into several: The Ante-Nicene Fathers, The Greek Fathers of the Golden Age, the Latin Fathers of the Golden Age, and seminars on an individual Father for qualified students at an advanced level. Ron took every course I offered. That was my specialty when I studied theology in France. When I came back, they needed somebody to teach that because there were few seminaries in the States with someone who was a specialist in that area. Usually, it would be taught by somebody who was a specialist in Scripture and would just "tag on" the Fathers. But I knew the Fathers, and that's what I taught: courses on the Fathers.

I think what really impressed Ron were the Cappadocians [Basil, Gregory of Nyssa, and Gregory of Nazianzus] because he told me it was from them he came to appreciate his own baptism and how he could help other people know what it meant to be baptized in Christ.

One day, Ron and I were talking about his plans for the "free" semester granted to students before ordination to the diaconate. A student could choose to do anything during his year in a parish. Ron told me he had always thought that an experience in another country would help him. An idea formed in my head. I asked him how well he knew French. He had studied it for two years in High School. I told him to check out a French Bible from the seminary library and begin reading his favorite Gospel. Then, he was to ask a classmate to help him read limited selections from other works in the Library on a regular basis. I would write to the Dean of Theology of the "Catho," as students called the Catholic University of Lyon, France, to design a program for Ron and plan for him to live with two university Professors, friends of mine. Expenses at the university would be less than in the States for Seminarians and I knew Georges and Henri would charge Ron nothing for room and board while introducing him to the intellectual and religious world of the city of St. Irenaeus. Years later, Ron told me that, as I spoke, he had only one thought in his head: "Either this woman is crazy or God has some plan that I don't know about yet." As we came to know Ron over the years, we know God had a plan.

Ron went to Lyon, studied, and lived with Henri and Georges, who, after they had retired from a teaching career, were called to the priesthood by the Cardinal Archbishop of Lyon. Ron returned to the States after a life experience that prepared him for what his life as a priest was to be.

I think it was from his own spirituality, and his own conviction that the people were part of what he was doing, that it wasn't just his "show." He spoke with me about ideas that he had and how he could put them into action in groups at the parishes. He had pastors when he was a young priest who encouraged him and understood that, too. So that was good.

He was a wonderful, blessed man. I was present at his ordination and his First Mass. He could do things to promote his own gifts. We stayed close friends.

His sudden death was a very hard thing for me because it was so unforeseen. I rarely cry, but I wept when I heard about his death.

Cardinal Blase Joseph Cupich

Archbishop of Chicago

Cardinal Blase Joseph Cupich was ordained to the priesthood in 1975, installed as the ninth Archbishop of Chicago in 2014, and elevated to Cardinal by Pope Francis in 2016.

Fr. Ron Lewinski was taken from us too soon.

At a critical moment in the renewal process of the Archdiocese of Chicago, I asked him to work with the Department of Parish Life and Formation. He responded positively with his characteristic generosity. Instead of moving toward retirement and fewer responsibilities, he willingly moved forward and into a complex new chapter of his ministry.

As I had watched him and had come to know him, I realized that he was the right person to give direction to our parish and formation initiatives. Obviously, his wide-ranging pastoral experiences equipped him well to take on these tasks. But there was something else that was decisively important. Fr. Ron was a life-long learner, someone who not only moved from experience to experience but who—with prayer and reflection—kept drawing on those experiences to learn new ways to serve God's people.

He was, in other words, a true disciple or learner, the kind who makes the best apostle in service to others.

Fr. Larry Dowling

Associate of Fr. Ron

Fr. Dowling received his Masters of Divinity (1991) and Doctor of Ministry (D. Min.) (1998) from the University of St. Mary of the Lake. He is a '97-'98 alumnus of Leadership Greater Chicago. He currently serves as Dean of Deanery III-D. He also serves as Board President for the ACTA Foundation and as Moderator for the Priests for Justice for Immigrants and as a Board member of the Augustus Tolton Pastoral Ministry Program at the Catholic Theological Union.

Ron asked me to join ACTA [Ed.—previously "Adult Catholic Teaching Aids" ACTA now stands for "A Commitment To All"] about three or four years before he died. Ron helped move things along at ACTA, things that were culturally innovative.

My experience with Ron at both ACTA and the Archdiocese is that he's highly respected, very thoughtful, very innovative, and also good with follow-through. You rarely find many people who have ideas and can actually put things into action. Ron was great at that.

He was involved with several initiatives on behalf of priests in the Archdiocese. The term used is "a priest's priest." He was definitely supportive of his brother priests, and very generous, sharing his wisdom, his time, and his talent.

I didn't get to know Ron real well until I came onto the ACTA Board and then the relationship became a lot more solidified, with a lot more insight into the many things that he was juggling and having success with.

He could challenge the powers that be when we, as Christians, are not being Christian. Ron had no problem doing that. He was very upfront, very forthright, but always in a way that wasn't an attack. It was 'think about this' or 'open yourself up to this possibility' or 'look at it this way.' He reinforced that in a lot of ways—a gentle, yet forceful, approach to ministry—just being clear. The clarity was rooted in faith and it was really evident in him.

He really helped move ACTA forward. I never felt like he was unprepared or entering into something unknown. He clearly had done his homework and wanted to make sure that if questions came up, he had thought about what a prospective grantee would do—those sorts of things.

I think there was a thoroughness and thoughtfulness about

everything he did. There was no question that Ron honored the past, the legacy. He would talk about legends of the Archdiocese who preceded all of us. He had that sense of honoring the past, but how do we take that into the future? How do we learn from that? What do we draw from that to move us forward?

He was great at knowing the history, knowing some dynamics of the presbyter and the diocese and the larger Church, and being able to bring that into a local perspective with things. That was definitely a genuine gift that he had.

He was doing his very best to bring to fullness the gifts that God gave him.

Carole Eipers

National Catechetical Consultant, William H Sadlier; ACTA Foundation Board Member
Director of the Office for Catechesis, Archdiocese of Chicago

Dr. Carole Eipers served in parish ministries for over twenty years as a teacher, Director of Religious Education, Youth Minister and Pastoral Associate. Carole was Director of the Office for Catechesis for the Archdiocese of Chicago for nine years and served as President of the National Conference of Catechetical Leadership. She has a Doctor of Ministry from Graduate Theological Foundation and a Master of Pastoral Studies from Loyola University.

I first met Ron when he was the Director of ODW, around 1989. I was on the staff of the office for catechesis. Then I became Director. We worked closely together. At first, I was rather in awe of him, because he was so known in the Archdiocese for his work in the Office for Divine Worship. He had collaborated on articles and books about liturgy, so I was very impressed to first meet him.

Then we started to work together. Ron had a wonderful depth of knowledge of liturgy, but he also appreciated that the formation that we did in catechesis was intimately connected to the people's ability to participate in the liturgy. When I was Director of Catechesis, he was Director of the worship office (ODW). We did several workshops together. He had a wonderful way of presenting. He would tell stories, but there was always his love for the liturgy and catechesis. He was very committed to working together and connecting the two.

The ODW tried to be faithful to what the Church was asking liturgy to be. People do not always like that. There is a joke: what's the difference between a liturgist and a terrorist? Well, you can negotiate with a terrorist. But he was not that way. He was not one of the liturgists who thought he knew everything. He would be open and listen to people, but still be faithful to what the Church was asking. A lot of people just don't like that.

The ODW was in charge of the major liturgy in the Archdiocese whether it was an ordination, or any number of things. Some people resisted the change, but there were just as many people applauding and thanking ODW for moving the Church the way it was supposed to move.

Regarding personal characteristics, the first thing that comes to me is his humility. He was kind and compassionate, and had a broader vision of Church than just 'my parish.'

Then faithfulness, certainly, not just to the liturgy but to his priesthood. Also, he always had a passion for ministry. He loved his ministry. Not just the liturgy, but whatever was involved— ministering to the people, being present with the people, trying to lead people, and to call forth people's gifts. I think the only way people are going to make a difference is if they find what they are passionate about. He had a passion.

Ron was sent by the Archdiocese to go to other countries to find excellent parishes with excellent liturgy. He went to several countries and gained tremendous insight.

He had a sense of humor. He had wisdom about the Church, about life, that he would share. I am impacted by his humility, but I just wish he hadn't taken it as far as he did.

Ron did a wonderful job running ACTA, and he brought wisdom. We have tons of proposals that come in. He would bring wisdom and a bigger sense of Church. We got some of these mission areas and he would say, well you know when I was in Africa this was a great need and we should consider a donation.

It was probably 2015 or 2016 when Ron and I were asked to speak in the United Arab Emirates at a conference. I had been there several times and this was Ron's first time. We were talking about liturgy and catechesis. We had a nice dinner and got on the plane. I realized my seat didn't recline. Now we're talking a long flight to Dubai and my seat would not recline. Ron had said through dinner and until we boarded, I'll never sleep, I never sleep on a plane. I said, I'm so lucky I can sleep anyplace anytime. Of course my seat would not recline and I complained to the stewardess and she explained she could do nothing about it.

Ron reclined, and slept the entire flight.

One thing I became aware of during his funeral was his mentoring of young priests. If you're in a role then somebody has to mentor. Inviting lay leadership and appreciating other people's gifts, and really calling them forth and affirming them. Which is hard to do when you don't feel affirmed yourself.

His expertise was internalized. He didn't just teach about the liturgy, he lived and loved the liturgy.

His impact on my life was appreciation for the liturgy in a different way.

Bishop Franz-Peter Tebartz-van Elst

Delegate for Catechesis in the Dicastery for Evangelization of the Roma Curia at the
  Vatican
Priest in Germany

Bishop Franz-Peter studied philosophy and Catholic theology at the Wilhelms University of Münster and the Albert-Ludwigs-University of Freiburg. He completed further theological studies at the University of Notre Dame in Indiana. From 1990 to 1996 he was vicar and chaplain at St. Paul's Cathedral in Münster, before receiving a teaching appointment at the University of Münster.

The first time I met Fr. Ron was on the day before the first Sunday of Lent in 1990. I came to the United States to do my doctoral dissertation on the RCIA. I came to Chicago to get in touch with the practical experiences of the RCIA. Fr. Ron introduced me to the catechuminates. So I still remember vividly when he took me to Holy Name Cathedral on the first Sunday of Lent. As head of the Office for Divine Worship, he was in charge of all the preparations and we had a wonderful celebration that afternoon. Between the celebrations, we were sitting together, reflecting on our experiences. That had been our first contact, and Fr. Ron introduced me to the inner dynamics of the liturgy in the pastoral context. I spent time with several parishes in Chicago that he had chosen to help me get in touch with the catechumenate in the parishes.

He seemed highly educated in liturgy, and he had got a genuine sense of the liturgical renewal of the Second Vatican Council. Not just what is sometimes a temptation regarding the liturgy—to make it an event or something like that, which is very popular in our times. But he really reflected in theological ways on the impact of the first constitution of the Second Vatican Council about liturgy. He could bring pride and a deep sense to everyone he was talking to, and bring also a sense of liturgy that you could feel. He was inspired, I think, in his ministry as the Director at ODW. The parishes were getting open to the sense of the Second Vatican Council.

My admiration increased over time because more and more I understood how deeply he understood the ideas of the Second Vatican Council. He was an advocate of good and deep liturgy; not just making entertainment for people, which I think is a big temptation in the United States, more than in Germany. He had been a wonderful advocate of the liturgical movement of the Second

Vatican Council.

He was deeply rooted in his spirituality. I had been fortunate to see how deeply he could pray; how much he got moved by praying, and also by praying for people.

He differed from other priests and pastors. That is really interesting because of how most of the people of his generation—we call them "68s" —are in a more ideological way. In Germany, it is a special expression—the "68 generation." It is a revolutionary society. The younger generation against the parents. The 1960s was a kind of restoration somehow. It was a change in democracy. The 1968 generation is a revolution against the traditional. In the United States, it was the Woodstock generation. Fr. Ron was from birth a member of this generation. But he never adopted that ideology. It distinguishes him from other priests of his generation. He had always been a man of the Second Vatican Council. That has been his theology. That has been his principle of teaching at Mundelein Seminary, which has brought him so close to the younger generation as well. He could understand them and build a bridge.

He was a very hospitable man when I was with him. When I was visiting him, he invited the bishop and priests for an evening of sharing. That has been very impressive to me.

He was someone who had very much gotten the metrics of this movement. He could relate to younger people, especially priests. He had a very good connection with the younger priests. He was teaching at the seminary in Mundelein, St. Mary of the Lake, and I think he was successful because he didn't judge people as belonging to special groups—left wing or right wing. His openness allowed him to transmit the inspiration of his age to another generation. He could listen to people and he had a gift of becoming close to people,

It does not happen in the Church as much as it should. So he was a kind of bridge building in the Church between generations. I think this explains how much they have accepted him in the Church of the Archdiocese of Chicago and below. He has given talks everywhere, and people have been able to recognize his authentic sense and his ability to build bridges. I think that is something very special about him. You won't find many priests who can do this because most of the "68s" are enraptured in ideology. He never has been captured by this.

I think Ron received very early the confidence of Cardinal Bernardin. So at a young age, he received an enormous responsibility in the Archdiocese of Chicago, and he has always been impressive in theology. He has not been a priest without theological reflection. That makes him interesting somehow for the younger generation. He has been able to dialogue in his teaching.

Because of his responsibility in the Archdiocese as Director of the ODW, pastor of St. Mary's Parish, and teaching at Mundelein Seminary, he always had contact with younger people. So that made it easier for him to get in touch with their thinking, to react, and to give them the theology of the Second Vatican Council. He had strong principles. He wasn't a man who just tried to be appropriate to the main stream. Not at all. He was a very reflective man about the theology of the Second Vatican Council, especially in terms of liturgy.

And for me, it is also very important, very convincing. I still remember talking with him after the death of Cardinal Bernardin. Archbishop George had been appointed. At the very beginning, he had been somewhat doubtful, but after they got in touch with each other—Cardinal George and himself—he became so close to Cardinal George. That shows his great personality: to be close to Cardinal Bernardin—who had differed greatly from Cardinal George —and to be close to Cardinal George. That it was possible was really great, really great. He has been so catholic in his thinking and feeling. He could give criticism to both, to Bernardin and to George, and they accepted him because of this. He had an honest personality.

He had the ability to listen, and that is very important. Ron didn't regard the young people as being an audience. He was listening, so he "got" the feeling of the younger generation and that made it possible for him to be a bridge to the younger generation. So many priests seem to listen, but for their interests. If they are for them they are priests, and if they are against them they refuse them. But Ron was listening with his heart. Watching what is going on, what is changing with the times. Also, I think his contact with nephews and nieces is very interesting, and very important, to get what is going on with the changing times.

He wasn't a pastor who was just a marionette of the parish. You will find these pastors as well. They will try to be close to the people but they don't have the courage and the skill to present themselves and their own position. He could listen. Not in a kind of dictatorship, but in a way to go on. A shepherd has to go on. I am from a rural area and I have had this discussion in my former diocese, where the shepherd always has to follow the sheep. But it isn't true. In nature, the shepherd has to go ahead with the sheep following. If there is a dangerous way, the sheep wouldn't go if the shepherd wouldn't go ahead. If you reach the other pasture, then you can let the sheep go. But people don't know the background of a shepherd. Ron has been a real Shepherd because he knew when to go ahead as the pastor leading, and when to let them go. That is very important for leadership.

Regarding the expansion at St. Mary's, I have only very positive memories. I visited with Fr. Ron several times. I could get something of the development and the great vision he had and he could somehow explain it to the parish. It was so convincing. Last week I visited it again and was so moved by what he'd been able to accomplish. I only have good memories of the St. Mary's project. I don't have any doubt about what has been developed there. I have been able to say Mass there several times and every time I realize how much that space works to bring people together. Also, he was so aware of the necessity for the adoration of the Eucharistic sacrament. The design of the Eucharistic Chapel shows his deep sense of, and closeness to, the sacrament and to the power of the priesthood.

Wilton Gregory [*], now Archbishop of Washington D.C., was a priest in the Archdiocese of Chicago. He did the First Rite of Election on the 4th of March, 1990. I realized how close he and Ron Lewinski were. Fr. Ron was always talking with great respect about Wilton Gregory. He's a very smart, sophisticated man with a doctoral thesis on liturgy. He was very close to Ron Lewinski because it was a topic they shared with each other.

There is a closing and clustering of parishes in Germany. It differs from diocese to diocese. Some parishes that have to do this get very, very big. Others are limited to a certain number of parishes. But it has to do with the fact that the small parishes can no longer survive because if you let them go, you have bad liturgy, bad preaching and music. So if they are together there is more possibility to have more quality. The people are no longer living close to just one place. Mobility has become more important. Modern people try to catch up with the Church not only in their parish, but in the hospital, the University, and churches more dedicated to certain types of holidays. So it is no longer just the place where you are living.

It is going on everywhere. When we started the process, they had used it in the United States, but for other reasons. The ethnic parishes from the time of immigration no longer made sense. In Germany, you never would find a church built in our rural landscape, where on the other side of the road there is a barn. In Germany, you have a more dense kind of population. Everything is very close together. So you would never build a church in a rural landscape because people would not show up. A church is always at the center of the population. In the United States, you have to provide for every purpose. Cardinal Bernardin knew who he could send.

Ron had such a strong personality. He also could react in a very emotional way. I realized that when he started tearing and crying. I realized there were great moments of joy but also great moments of sorrow. I know that the whole process of building the church had not been easy for him. When I was visiting the place in April, it was so interesting where they had put the bench that he had been sitting at. I realized that this was the place where he had been aware of all the difficulties and obstacles when building the church. He was proud about the project.

Then he had been called by Cardinal Cupich [*] to take over this new mission for parish vitality. One day, I met with Cardinal Cupich in Rome, and immediately he started talking about Fr. Ron. The Cardinal said to me, "He is such a good priest."

Ron could be open to every new collaborator. For example, Fr. Peter Wojcik [*] as co-director. And Fr. Andrew Liaugminas [*], who is also a very reflective man and gave a wonderful homily at Ron's funeral. I think that he is proof, or a sign, of how Ron had reached out to a younger generation. Fr. Andrew is a very intellectual man. And Fr. Robert Fedek [*] is a different person as well. All these priests that I have met have been such a gift to me when I was visiting Ron. We had wonderful conversations, sharing around a big table.

He had a very pious, let us say, way of celebrating the Mass. When he was at St. Theresa [after St. Mary's], we would say Mass together in the morning on weekdays. The way he prepared for every celebration of the Mass so deeply, so personally, impressed me very much. I think it is about the preparation, about how someone behaves in the sacristy. Is he focused on what he is doing, or is it just a job where he talks to everyone? He was kind to everyone who showed up; but in preparing for the Mass, the last minutes were minutes between God and him. He looked at everything so that they had prepared it in the right way, that it would be worthy for liturgy.

The liturgy was adopted by the Second Vatican Council; it was the focus of all that he did. I did a feature on German radio about my visit to St. Mary's for the groundbreaking in 2000. It had been prepared so well by him, and it has moved me so much, the procession from the gym, past the old church, past the cemetery with all the German names of the original settlers, and then down to the field where the groundbreaking service took place.

To me, Fr. Ron was a role model for the priesthood. We, of course, have known many priests over our lives, but Fr. Ron was different. The older generation of priests were somehow the father of the parish. The young ones have not been able to take over the role of a father. Some have not experienced a father in their own families from whom they had learned what a father is about. Fr. Ron had. He could build the bridge from one generation in history to the next one. I think that is the main focus of the witness that he has given to the Church. He has been the linking element of two very different faces in Church history.

He has somehow created the future of the Church. Even the building of the church is something that is leading people into the future. The concept of the church is totally the concept of liturgy and theology of the Second Vatican Council. I have been impressed so much by the chapel of adoration. It shows how important the Eucharistic sacrament was for him. Otherwise, he would not have put so much focus on the space. Some priests regard themselves as the entertainer for the parish; they wouldn't put so much focus on the chapel of adoration. It is actually proof of the theology. Like a temple. It is open to everybody. You can find it. It is not hidden.

The whole concept of the church, the baptismal font, and the narthex, is so great—and how they used the narthex at his funeral to display memorabilia from his life. He had the concept of the church that is about what you can see. One evening we came back from a meeting and saw the church illuminated. It is very very special.

There were so many people at his funeral that took place in the sanctuary; and also in the narthex. That shows he had a great vision of the church and he was able to fill it with faith and with people. I have never experienced a funeral with so many priests attending. Incredible. The Cardinal, the bishops, you will never find this. Even at bishops' funerals. So many identified as priests, and all generations.

It is a kind of heritage to the whole diocese because he already was talking about how a church could be or should be before he built a church. When he had an opportunity to build one, it was a real blessing because he expressed what he had been teaching. It doesn't matter whether or not he had been a pastor before. His whole life from Vatican II through ordination and everything he did leading up to that had prepared him. I think he was the perfect person. Probably it was good that he hadn't been a pastor before, so as not to be spoiled by "daily business." Instead, from his ministry as Director of ODW, he came into a situation where he had to shape a parish in totally new ways. That is a special grace. He came with more attention, with more awareness, not doing "business as usual" as if he'd done it before, which is usually the case. He could use his personal strengths. In a way, it was a situation where Cardinal Bernardin said, "Show us what you've learned. We're going to send you out there. Build that parish and show me what you've learned."

Ron was very much shaped by liturgy, and he educated me. We were very close and shared experiences in Rome, Greece, Germany, and the United States. He liked to travel, and he liked to make presentations everywhere. He had a broad sense of bringing in aspects of other cultures and other perspectives.

He had a great impact on me.

Pat & Donna Fahey

Pat passed into eternity in 2020.
Friends of Fr. Ron beginning with his first parish, St. Frances of Rome in Cicero, IL

We met Ron the very first day that he was at St. Frances of Rome, his first parish after ordination. We were having the Holy Name Society meeting and Ron came over to the meeting and spoke to us and we got to at least know that he was the new Associate Pastor at the parish. From that day on, we became very good friends with Fr. Ron. We have five children altogether and they were in school. He became almost like a part of our family.

We got to know him quite well. Then, as he became more involved in liturgy, he invited us to become part of the liturgy committee at the parish. One time he talked about his experience the first time he had gone to Gethsemani for a retreat and how that developed. I mentioned I was supposed to go there when I was in high school when they opened the retreat house. So he said, well, why don't we go out and do that?

I was teaching in Chicago Public Schools and we decided that during my Spring break, we would go to Gethsemani. We went there every year thereafter for at least twenty-five years, with a minor break. We traveled to Gethsemani always during Spring break. There was a time when they closed their Retreat House because they were redoing it, so we went to St. Myron's in Indiana. Another time we went to the Abbey outside of Rochester, NY. So we always went some place on retreat, the two of us.

Sometimes we would deviate on the way back from Gethsemani and go to places where he'd heard they were building a church. One was in Frankfurt, Kentucky. Another in a town near Paducah. So we visited those places and Ron would get some ideas. He was always on the lookout for something that he could incorporate into St. Mary's.

When Ron first learned about Gethsemani, he would have missed Merton. One of Ron's good friends, Fr. Dan Coughlin—used to go to Gethsemani as well, and he knew Merton. Fr. Dan became the first Catholic chaplain, the 59th Chaplain of the U.S. Congress. He and Ron were good friends.

We started going to Gethsemani around 1974-75. We hardly missed a year after that. The last time we went was around 2016. By then he was no longer pastor at St. Mary—he was working in the Archdiocese. He was always traveling and doing all kinds of things. He said he was tired and wanted to get away and rest for a while. So we went to Gethsemani. It was about a year before he died.

Ron was kind of high-strung. He worried a lot about things. A retreat put him in a different frame of mind—relaxed him. Normally, after the evening meal, we'd take a little walk out into the woods. We would spend maybe an hour just talking before coming back for the last hour. Every evening we would take these walks through the woods; it was always really nice. We talked about many things: politics, things in the Church, and our families. He'd often talk about his own family, his sister, and his brother-in-law. Eventually, we got to know his parents and his family quite well, too. We traveled with them and had parties with them. He would talk about them a lot. He would talk about his years in the seminary, anything that interested him—and that was quite a bit. It was a way for him to unwind about things.

The Abbey has a tremendous amount of land. Once, we were walking along the road and we saw a monk all by himself out in the field. He had a golf club, and he was hitting imaginary golf balls. The monk said, "One thing I always envisioned about this monastery is that they could turn part of it into a golf course." He loved golf, so he'd come out there to practice his swing. We thought it was funny to think about turning the place into a golf course.

Another time, within the last ten years the monks invited Ron to come down and give a series of talks to them. He called me and said, "What are you doing? Can you go with me? I've talked to a lot of people around the world; but for me to go to these monks for a series of talks, I'm just rattled right now." He was so worried about it and he asked me to come with him and give him moral support. I went down, and the Abbot allowed me to sit in with the monks as Ron gave his talks. After the first one, he asked "Well, how did I do?" I said, "Well, they seemed to be attentive: they were listening." Ron was worried that he would not go over very big with the monks at Gethsemani.

They wanted to hear about things in general about the liturgy. The liturgy at the Abbey is quite different. I'll never forget the first time I went down there. The music was different; it was uplifting, and we looked forward to it. There was an organist who also wrote music. He was really wonderful.

Ron was in Lyon, France for about three months. And he'd been to Poland too. Sr. Agnes Cunningham [*], in her order, had a place in Lyon. In fact, Ron and I went to Lyon one time. We walked around and he reminisced and told us some stories about when he'd been there before. He told us this story about when he and a local man he'd gotten to know walked around and Ron said "Hey, how old do you think this building is?" and the man said "Oh, let me see. This is one of the young buildings: maybe five or six hundred years."

Pastor Joe Howard at St. Frances was very open to things. So he'd listen to Ron. There was another priest who taught at Loyola University. They were all very open to Vatican II. Fr. Howard was in his fifties. He had two brothers who were also priests. He'd been resident in Rome for some time and they appointed him pastor at St. Frances. He was a great guy, and Ron really appreciated him.

Another person who was a big influence on Ron was John Canary [*]. John was originally at St. Frances as a deacon, and he and Fr. Howard were very close friends. After ordination, they assigned him to a parish on the south side; but he was still very close to what was happening at St. Frances.

When Fr. Ron came to St. Frances, the liturgy was not up to par in a lot of ways. He had learned about the liturgy and the changes that were taking place. He incorporated that into life at the parish. We would go once or twice a year with other people to a place in Geneva, Illinois and we would spend a day there and just relax and talk about improving the liturgy at St. Frances. The place allowed us to use their facility and their swimming pool. Ron loved to swim.

At St. Frances, he did all kinds of things. We started a program at the beginning of Lent called "Ashes to Easter." Ron had home Masses. We set up committees where we would go out to people and use their homes to have Mass and afterward talk about the liturgy and things they understood about the Church and so forth. That was always interesting.

Ron incorporated a lot in terms of music, and study groups, and got more things going on. It was amazing. They all came from him. He was just brilliant in a lot of things. He was very much into the music. That's why, when he headed upped the liturgical commission for the Archdiocese, that's what he did. He went to a few parishes as an Associate, and eventually, he just resided in the parish where he worked.

Ron traveled to a lot of places worldwide. His reputation became international. He was invited to speak in different places. I know he spoke in Germany, Poland, and a lot of places, about liturgical things.

He was a very devout and dedicated priest. He believed deeply in the priesthood and the Church. Despite what many people would say about scandals and all that, he never lost faith in the Church. With all its shortcomings, he still had a deep reverence for the Church and all that it stood for.

I've known Ron since July 1972. We've done a lot together; celebrated our birthdays; so much. Ron took us to many places. We were in Rome for his 25th anniversary of priesthood [1997]. We went to Switzerland; all over Europe. We took a three-week tour through Europe with him. He introduced us to a lot of things that we would never have thought about regarding the Church. He was very bright.

We were shocked when he died. We couldn't believe it.

Prior to coming to St. Mary's, he'd met the right people, no doubt about it, to help him. He was the right person at the right time for that job.

Fr. Robert Fedek

Priest Secretary to Cardinal Cupich
Former Associate Pastor at Saint Mary of the Annunciation

Father Robert Fedek was ordained to the priesthood in 2005. He served as associate pastor at Saint Mary of the Annunciation Parish from 2005 to 2010.

I got to know Fr. Ron when I was studying; he was not teaching when I was at Mundelein Seminary. We had a different teacher for liturgy; but sometimes Ron would come for lectures.

He was charismatic, and yet he was restrained. He was outgoing when he needed to be. He was also introverted. That was interesting. He had a complex personality. When he needed to be loud or to make his point he was not shy to make his point or to challenge.

Regarding his passing, I look at it more from the spiritual point of view, and I look for the direct benefit for Fr. Ron. When you step back and reflect on who we are as followers of Jesus you know that we are on the way home. When you look at Fr. Ron's life and his spirituality, he was such a generous man and priest, and from that point of view he completed himself. As an Archdiocesan he was a liturgist for years; that was his passion. He loved liturgy. So he could influence at that particular time during Cardinal Bernardin. He had a chance to become a pastor and he fulfilled himself in that aspect as well by creating wonderful community and building a beautiful church giving us hope and practicing what he believed. Then he was again invited to be part of the Archdiocese to create a new pastoral approach for parishes, with Parish Transformation looking differently at pastoral life in the present context. He continued to help parishes go through that transition. Then that became the spark for Renew My Church. The pastoral layer of that really grew out of Parish Transformation.

So you see how tremendously he influenced the Church in Chicago in a quiet and humble way; and serving on many different committees. He helped run the Office of Mission and Vitality during his last year. He really completed himself in that way. There really was not much more except becoming a bishop, but only so many people can be ordained to episcopacy.

So if you look at his spiritual journey and his pastoral accomplishments he achieved retirement age but he still continued to be involved. He became what I think of as a senior advisor for the Archdiocese and Cardinal. He could still do a lot; but with age, the problems begin. He was probably starting to experience some of that; he was quiet about it. And my point of view is if he was going to continue, but starting to struggle with his health in years to come, then this would limit his ability. He was on fire. He was a workaholic. He would never sit down. I think in those circumstances he would suffer.

I think maybe God rewarded him by saying "You know, you did so much for the Church, come to a better place; I'm saving you from the cross of aging and possibly suffering." You know, this is my own spiritual take on it. When you look at it that way, God took him home. What else, from a spiritual point of view, can you dream of? It's really the perfect dream. Be involved to the end, accomplish great things, and go home with no regrets.

We won't remember this great man as someone who became fragile and unable to continue. So from that perspective I see it as a blessing. But you really have to be spiritual and be happy for him. I don't think he wants us to have any regrets. Because if we dwell on him, honestly from a selfish point of view, we want to keep him forever because he was so great. For me, it is much easier to accept his passing because I knew him and I know he's happy now.

And what I would add to that from my personal point of view is that I believe he continues to live in us and through us, through the wonderful moments that we experienced together that we'll always cherish in our hearts and minds. But even more important the values, the thoughts, the challenges, the questions that he asked, the directions that he invited us to go, the dreams to pursue. I think that all of that is enough, at least to me, as a young priest asking him a lot of questions and following his example, work hard, being generous, not holding anything back.

I think in that way he continues to live in me. I think it is beautiful. Now I need to believe in myself because I cannot just go back to him by making a phone call. I believe that what he already instilled me has to bear fruit, almost like I have to graduate and believe in myself. Do it on my own. And because of the circumstances now I have to do it; I'm almost forced to do it, because I cannot rely on him. So its like jumping into deep water. Before, I was resistant to swimming because I could depend on Fr. Ron. But now he says, no, you have to do it; you know how to do it. Go!

In that way, I think he continues to live in us. We are like his legacy. The values we live in, and the Church, how we understand it and the community. And remember his missions, retreats, lectures on liturgy and RCIA across the world. He touched the hearts of many, internationally: Germany, Australia, Malaysia.

The parish at St. Mary's has such a treasure because of the energy, sacrifice, and dedication of Fr. Ron's leadership and the good people that he was able to energize to move forward with that project. It takes a charismatic leader to direct that energy.

When you look at the whole life of Fr. Ron you begin to see how pieces of the puzzle come together and lead to something bigger. Certainly, I'll miss him; and it was hard to accept the fact that he is "gone." But we know that he is with us in spirit. I feel that, and I continue to do my ministry. Quite often I call on the pastoral insights that he gave me over the years.

I miss him. Sometimes I'm ready to pick up the phone and call him. I think that he's on a trip somewhere and he'll come back.

When you look at Fr. Ron's life and his spirituality, he was a quiet saint.

Deacon Howard Fischer

Deacon at St. Mary of the Annunciation
Friend of Fr. Ron

I first met Ron Lewinski at a wedding in Michigan in 1984. He was the celebrant, and I was a groomsman. We met at the rehearsal and clicked instantly. We shared a passion for pastoral ministry and for the liturgy, but our connection went way beyond common interests. I just loved the man as a human being and I loved his approach to his priestly ministry, and I greatly respected his great intellect and wisdom. Ron put up with my sarcasm and I enjoyed his dry, witty one-liners. We became friends from that weekend on. And while the frequency of our dinners and phone conversations varied over the middle decades of our friendship, the bond never lessened.

Ron was brilliant—not just with academic knowledge (which wasn't limited to theology) but he also possessed an incredible intuition about people and situations. He could detect things going on and he was always spot-on. One thing I sorely miss is his wisdom and advice.

As a priest, Ron was humble and compassionate, and very pastoral. Because, by his own admission, he was very introverted, Ron was uncomfortable in crowds of people. His forte was not idle chitchat and backslapping. But one-on-one and in small groups, he was very warm and insightful. And he had a great sense of humor.

Because he thought before he spoke, Ron's words always had great wisdom and power. His ability to make friends and keep in contact with them was amazing. For someone who was a professed introvert, Ron had more real friends than a hundred extroverts added together! How he found the time and energy in his very busy life to frequently connect with all these friends is still a mystery to me.

A particular gift Ron had was his amazing ability to see the proverbial big picture and envision new realities. He could see and describe new futures, and new ways of doing things, and enlist people in the cause. While many of us get comfortable with the status quo or can only think in terms of incremental change, Ron's vision was transformational.

The impact that Ron had on my life (and on my family) is huge.

The richness of our friendship, his advice and insights, his hiring me at St. Mary's, and traveling to the Holy Land and Italy... are all just a few pieces of a galaxy of highlights and events that profoundly shaped my life.

Affection for Ron extended to my children, particularly my son, Matt. Matt and his fiancé Neely went to Ron for marriage prep when they felt that what they received elsewhere was incomplete. They later shared more than a few dinners together. When Matt moved into his new home a few years ago, literally the first thing he did was to tape Ron's prayer card to the front of his fridge, just like in our house.

Ron was humble and loathe to toot his own horn. However, he was quietly proud of some things he accomplished in his ministry. There's a lot to pick from, but one that stands out is that he was very proud of having Pope John Paul II conduct the Rite of Reception at the Mass in Grant Park in 1979. The RCIA rituals, which Ron had a hand in developing, were new and it was the first time a pope had celebrated any of them.

When he died, my wife Maryann and I commented about how many blessings we had in our life that resulted from our relationship with Ron. It was (and is) amazing.

Roger Fisher

Entrepreneur
Parishioner and supporter of the Pastor at St. Mary's parish

Whether it is business, parish, or family, Roger is a strong supporter of others while helping them achieve success. He and his wife Jacqueline, were the donors of the superior pipe organ at St. Mary's parish.

I do what I learned from my father when it came to the Church and the pastor: my job is to support the pastor. No one ever goes to him just to say "you're doing a great job" or "how are you." They always have something on their minds. And he has the right as a pastor to be wrong. But my job is to support his decisions. Every pastor at St. Mary's was the right guy at the right time, without a doubt. Every one of them.

If I ever had a problem with Fr. Ron, it was that he never thought he did the job well enough. He always thought he could do better. I said that's nice, but you know what? You have to enjoy things as they come. He was never happy with himself.

He was a great author and a good friend. But he wasn't comfortable being praised.

As soon as we said we were going to build a church, I said, okay I want to pay for the organ. I had a little experience at St. Joseph's downtown in Chicago on Orleans Street. The pastor there was my teacher. I went to a boarding school, St. Bede's, in Peru, Illinois. They had an organ, and the church has unbelievable art in it. I was at Mass there one time and I looked up and way in the back was this huge organ. I said, Father, why don't you play that? He said, well, it was damaged during the lightning storm. So we interviewed a few people, and I found a company to rework the whole thing.

There are usually three to five people that work on organs. Now there are big companies that make cookie cutters, but this type of organ at St. Mary's is the best. That was in the design from the beginning because there was going to be an organ loft. What is different is that the pipes you see actually play, they are not ornamental. There is nothing ornamental about anything on that organ.

One problem that occurred during the parish expansion is that the Archdiocese had a lot of things that they wanted Fr. Ron to do.

So he was absent a lot of time. Many people didn't like that.

I found Ron's ability to teach bishops to be an anomaly. They would ask him how to be a bishop.

A big thing for Sr. Gael Gensler [*] was to grow the ministries, which she did very well. She was another great asset. An unbelievable person.

One lighthearted moment I remember is when someone asked the architect, Dirk Lohan [*], the question, "Have you ever built a church before?" and he answered, "No, but I never built a bad one."

When Fr. Ron arrived and talked about change, I said this is the right time for it. I thought they sent him here to get it going and then someone else would step in. I was surprised that he stayed as long as he did.

Sr. Gael Gensler

Pastoral Associate at St. Francis of Assisi Parish
Pastoral Associate at St. Mary of the Annunciation from 1997 to 2003

Sr. Gael Gensler became a beloved staff member at St. Mary of the Annunciation and was the primary force behind the development of ministries there.

I was working in Wichita Kansas and my community wanted me to go back to the Midwest to do formation work. They agreed that I could continue to do ministry as well because at that point they had somebody in formation. So I contacted Ron to see if he knew of any parishes in the area that needed that. He said, "Yes I do, right here." So that is literally how it happened. It was that simple. I was looking for a job and he was looking for pastoral associate. I started in 1997. I was there six years. My job was to help bridge the old and the new.

In some ways we chose not to do too much with the ministries at the old church. But after Mass at Diantha Hall we recruited all kinds of people. So when we were ready to move to the new church we had a whole cadre of new people. There wasn't any youth ministry. That was one of the first things that I started, to initiate some kind of gathering for teens. We had our first teen mission trip to Monessen, Pennsylvania. There were three teens and three adults. The next year we got twelve. And after that we had forty. Several parishioners were involved.

The other team that Ron wanted me to work with was the RCIA. At that point the couple leading it wanted to step down so I needed to recruit some people to help. I recruited [parishioner] Al Dietz before he was in the deacon program, and I recruited [parishioner] Kathi Barrett [*]. I also started women's retreats.

Developing the parish mission statement was a collaborative effort. It described a Vatican II parish, but it was very much from the people. That took time. We worked on that at the parish—but we met at the seminary.

Chicago was the premier liturgy office. It was the number one liturgy office in the U.S. When Ron was in charge of it, everybody looked to Chicago. They studied the documents of the Second Vatican Council. They knew exactly what they wanted to do in order to make that happen in the Archdiocese. The tabernacle was not to be on the altar. The tabernacle was not to be in the main place. Their focus was on the Liturgy of the Word.

Ron started the Chicago Catechumenate magazine. He was known worldwide for that.

Ron recognized his gifts, but he also recognized his limitations. He was not comfortable doing fundraising. He didn't like asking people for money. He was not good at chitchat. So after Mass on weekends he was exhausted if he did that. He was a strong introvert. Those were his limitations and he knew it.

I liked every aspect of the work at St. Mary's. There wasn't only one area. It was good to grow the RCIA because Ron knew the Rites and Jim Scavone [*] knew the music for the Rites so we could celebrate liturgy well. When you have those elements it makes a big difference.

Bishop John Gorman

Auxiliary Bishop Emeritus of the Chicago Archdiocese
Rector at Mundelein Seminary, 1966-1973

Most Rev. John Gorman, D.D. was the fourth Rector of Mundelein Seminary. He was ordained to the priesthood in 1952. Previously, he served as a faculty member of the Archdiocese of Chicago's high school and college seminaries, Loyola Pastoral Studies Institute, and Notre Dame University Summer School.

The seminary prior to Vatican II was a very regimented kind of life. Everyone was judged by their life in the seminary. The whole idea was that the seminary reflected the Church, which was really in a defensive mode because of the revolutions of the 16th and 17th centuries. So the Church was supposed to be apart from the world, and therefore the seminaries were to be apart from the world physically and in every other way. That was true also of Mundelein.

We never got out of the building until after Christmas for a vacation. For ordination, you were judged by how you lived your life in the seminary. There was no contact with "outside" people.

They appointed me Rector right after Vatican II ended. It became clear that the Council changed the way the Church saw itself. Instead of being apart from the world, it began to see itself as in dialogue with, and of service to, the world. The word that Vatican II sent to seminaries was that the seminary should change and follow the mission of the Church. So there's a lot of change.

The seminary before Vatican II was encapsulated in fear: you wouldn't dare break a seminary rule. So now we loosened up the whole seminary, with students going out into parishes. These are men in their twenties. In the "outside world," some of them would probably be married. So I gave them the idea of "responsible freedom." That's exactly what they're going to have to be responsible for at the parish: how they handle their freedom. It was abused by some, and others came to realize what it meant.

Theology didn't really have a pastoral dimension about the people—how the seminarians are going to serve their parishes. Sacred Scripture was to be read according to modern literary expertise. And the programs and expectations weren't well related, so you have seminarians going out to parishes in various ways, living with and serving parishes. So, for ordination, the input from parishes became part of the evaluation of the seminarian—what the people thought of him.

The seminary building in the old days was a place of complete silence. Once you entered, you would not talk in the building, and you were never allowed to visit a seminarian's room. That's one of the things we changed. There were ten men living in a corridor. So we opened it up into a group, having meetings and sharing experiences, and praying together. We changed the whole idea of being apart from each other to being with and for each other. A parish priest was trained in group dynamics and we had him in the corridor where these ten men lived. So they were no longer living apart from the world or apart from each other. That's the overall view of how and why these changes at the seminary took place—because the Church was changing.

Some of the faculty were older man and they didn't like all the changes. We had a faculty meeting and one of the famous teachers —a Jesuit—asked, "Is the new rector now about to change our authority?" I said, "According to Vatican II, we're not changing authority. We are changing the way authority is meant to be operative."

Ron was obviously very bright and interested in liturgy and leadership. I think he had the ability to convince people by the integrity of his whole life, the ability to respect other people with whom he was living, and share and engage in the work that he was committed to.

After he was ordained, he became very important for the whole diocese in developing liturgy—how liturgy is meant to be part of a parish. He developed a lot of programs. I had great respect for him. We were friends.

We were all very much appreciative of what Ron did. He was a nice smiley guy. He brought liturgy alive.

Cardinal Wilton Daniel Gregory

Archbishop of Washington D.C.
Fellow liturgical expert and friend of Fr. Lewinski

Cardinal Wilton Daniel Gregory began his career as a priest in the Archdiocese of Chicago, having been ordained one year after Fr. Lewinski. After ordination, he completed a doctorate in sacred liturgy (SLD) at the Pontifical Liturgical Institute at the Pontifical Atheneum of St. Anselm in Rome. He taught at Saint Mary of the Lake Seminary and served as a master of ceremonies under Cardinals Cody and Bernardin. He was the first Black president of the United States Conference of Catholic Bishops (USCCB) from 2001 to 2004. Pope Francis elevated him to the rank of Cardinal on November 28, 2020. He is the first African-American Cardinal.

Fr. Ron Lewinski was a wonderful priest and cherished colleague. His devotion to priestly ministry was exemplary and his dedication to liturgical excellence was widely known and deeply appreciated.

Ed Hendricks

President & CEO of Dynamic Developments Training & Leadership
Parishioner and President & CEO of Dynamic Developments Training & Leadership

Prior to founding Dynamic Developments, Ed spent nearly a decade with AT&T Corporate Education and Training. He then became VP of Streetsmart Concepts Inc., a training company. Ed applies his skills to organizational consulting/coaching, custom development and delivery of training, and 360° upward feedback analysis and facilitation. He and his wife Cynthia were active in ministries at St. Mary's parish. They have five children.

Fr. Ron reached out to me because of the training I do for a living. He and I spent many, many hours while the church was being built, walking through the skeleton of a building. He was extremely analytical, very soft-spoken, and he knew what he wanted. He was mild-mannered and he explained his reasoning behind why he wanted certain things.

All my training is around behavior. Fr. Ron is what I would call an Expressive Analytical, "analytical" being his dominant style. He had a vision, but he was really focused on the details to make certain that it was correct. He wanted the path to the entrance to be a walkway into the church. That, and Emmaus Drive, should prepare you to serve the Lord in church. He wanted everyone to walk down a path and, as they walked, forget everything on their minds and think about where they are going—they are going to church, and they're going to honor our Lord and Savior, Christ. So when we go to church, we make certain we walk down that path as a reminder.

"I want everyone to feel welcome," he'd say. That struck me and always stayed with me.

There is a lot of uniqueness to that church. Before parishioners saw anything, he envisioned it. We would walk through this empty shell and we'd stop—and this is where his expressive side came out—he got all excited and would say this is where this or that is going to be. The man had a passion for detail, even down to the windows being different sizes. They're going to be different sizes because all kinds of people will walk into this church; that's what he wanted them to signify. He had thoughts about how they were positioned so they wouldn't be uniform because people aren't uniform. The stations of the cross are off to the side, so your total focus is on Jesus and the walk to his crucifixion.

Many people didn't think he was very creative, but he was

extremely creative. The baptismal font is one of my favorites. When you first enter the sanctuary you to dip a finger in the font's holy water and, while making the sign of the cross, we commit ourselves and washing our sins away. He designed it to be tomb-like because of Paul's writings. John submerged Jesus, and the Holy Spirit descended upon him when he came out of the water. Ron wanted the font to signify that. The meaning behind total submersion is that as you go in you're leaving your old life behind; and when you come out, you're inviting the Holy Spirit into your heart.

He had the vision and wanted to reflect the liturgy. Regarding the base of the steeple inside the sanctuary, every time I'm at church, I envision Jesus rising and returning for the final judgment. The only thing we were disappointed with was that the cross on top of the spire, not just the spire, was supposed to light up so you could see it from everywhere.

What I teach all over the world is that the best leaders are the most versatile leaders. It is a shame that some people didn't get to know him better. In my mind, he was one of the most versatile world leaders that I ever met. His dominant style was definitely analytical; but when the situation called for it, he could be a driving-analytical, expressive-analytical, or amiable-analytical.

The man on the outside was very stoic and detail-oriented, very monotone; but behind all of that was great reasoning.

In 2003, Fr. Ron asked me to come in and train prior to the school year starting. We had all the teachers, and we had Fr. Sal (Associate Pastor), Sue Matousek [*] (Director of Religious Education), Victoria Hansen (Administrative Assistant), Debbie Dedeo (School Principal), etc. The number one thing on his list was when we get together, we're going to pray together. Something that was really important to him was that he's upfront with his expectations of the entire staff. He told me, I expect everyone here to serve with a pastoral heart and pastoral attitude. We are called to shepherd God's people and not to produce programs or events for our own sake. He expected every staff member to present themselves —and he had this expectation of himself as well—at an event that was going to affect everyone at the parish.

He wanted it to be evident to the parishioners that everything to do with the Church and the staff was about working in solidarity with one another. That was huge to him. We just can't afford to be sloppy or second-rate.

The Hertel Family

Parishioners

The Hertel's are descendants of one of the founding families of St Mary of the Annunciation Parish.

Our family of six children calls St. Mary's our spiritual home. We were formed and shaped here with the love and guidance of so many, especially Fr. Ron Lewinski. Many times he shared our table where our children sometimes called him Uncle Fr. Ron. We enjoyed his invitations to travel on pilgrimages, the Abbey of Gethsemani for retreats, Mission trips in Belize, and many more "God Moments" throughout our twenty-one-and-a-half years with him.

He freely gave of himself in visits and notes. He could write a small note with a big impact. I looked forward to his Christmas card each year. That is where he would reaffirm his gratitude for our friendship of loyalty, trust, and respect.

From his first days at the parish, I knew he was planning something wonderful for St. Mary's. He impressed me as focused, enthusiastic, and ready to lead our parish to fulfill the Mission of Christ. He had diverse ways of inviting people to this mission: some direct, but more often with subtle nudges.

At his first parish meeting in the little church basement, I signed up to be on a "committee" to reorganize the then rectory into an office space. During that project, I realized this new friendship was a gift but certainly did not know at the time how it would grow to be so deeply treasured. I remember telling him I believed God puts some people in our lives for a long time and some are just passing through. So I asked him if he was going to "run off" on us and become a bishop; to which he quickly laughed. His quick wit, humor, and genuine honesty in this new relationship intrigued me and soon our trust developed.

When Fr. Ron came to St Mary, he was living near the Mundelein Seminary for the previous year, as he was on sabbatical. His appointment was a time of transition for him without an adequate place of residence. Our family was in transition too, as we were planning to build our dream house on the lake. As both of our housing situations developed, we had opportunities to learn more about each other.

He freely put himself "out there" for people and developed beloved friendships. There were other times his feelings would be hurt, and times he suffered betrayal. He trusted my family and me with that vulnerability for years to come. It formed the foundation of love and respect. Our gratitude for his love and friendship in our lives grew as we raised our children, buried our parents, and enjoyed the many ways we learned to strive to be good stewards and mission disciples. He was there with us at our most desperate times, as well as the many celebrations and milestones. He brought his stories, encouragement, humor, and wit to our family table on many Sunday evenings. God knows he didn't come for my cooking. We knew he came for the "safe harbor" and "loyal friendship" that we know he shared with many other families as well. We learned so much from his example of trust, respect, honesty, and faith. We are all a work in progress. Yes, our family felt special.

His friendship came with a responsibility, too. Fr. Ron was a gift to our family, which we chose to accept and treasure. He gave us his vulnerability, and we gave him respect. He gave us his trust, and we gave him our loyalty. He gave us a listening heart, and we gave him a family. It's not much different from our call from Christ to love and accept His love and trust that gift to grow with you to eternal life. There is still great pain from his passing, but we find comfort in treasured memories and the kindness of others. He continues to be a gift to our family. I could write a book about Fr. Ron in our lives, but it couldn't be published because loyalty and confidentiality cannot be separated, just like love and forgiveness.

Through many conversations, experiences, our Sunday suppers, and Sacred Liturgies, Fr. Ron taught me to listen with my heart and see people with a wider vision and at the same time, to be open to an encounter with someone as a visit with Christ. He would share what gave him great joy, as well as some of what he feared. He told me of his wishes for his final earthly resting place. There was never any doubt that he loved the Church of Christ and he served faithfully with his whole heart.

Fr. Ron's love of the sacraments never took a back seat. We learned this when our youngest was preparing for his first reconciliation. One evening when Fr. Ron walked in the back door for Sunday supper, he was immediately given a chair by our son who said, "Father, sit down so I can practice my confession." So right there in the kitchen, he began. When it came time to name his sins, our son said, "My sins are blah, blah, blah" and continued with his confession. I watched quietly as Fr. Ron held back some laughter and quickly said, "Well, I think it's time to absolve your sins."

We were blessed to bring our daughter Allison on one of the pilgrimages with Father. Anyone who's traveled with Fr. Ron through an airport knows two things; he walked super-fast, and his favorite airport word was "flughafen." Fr. Ron did not know that Allison was a bit timid of escalators and needed help to get on them. As we came to a three-story escalator, she suddenly stopped. Seeing her fear, he turned off his rush and very naturally took her hand and helped her get on. His compassionate response made Allison feel at ease and we all made it to our flight. On the last day of this pilgrimage, we were all together for our farewell dinner. Fr. Ron and Allison were sitting across the table from me and Joe. As each large plate of pig knuckles was served, Allison's eyes grew wider and more confused. When her plate was placed in front of her, she gasped and quietly said to Father I don't know how to eat this. Again, he casually took up her knife and fork and cut the meat off for her.

Fr. Ron was a man who was honest with his emotions. I saw times that brought him to tears. I saw times he painfully held back his tears. I know he was sensitive and stubborn many times; but he lived with an extra serving of humility. He shared his quick wit, laughter, and good sense of humor. One year at our Thanksgiving table, as we shared our gratitude, he listened to my little granddaughter thank God for her new baby in Mommy's tummy. As joy erupted at the announcement, I saw happy tears in Uncle Fr. Ron's eyes. He lived with a faithful, humble, servant's heart and shared that life as a member of our family. He is a gift.

He came to St Mary the year our fourth child was to receive the First Eucharist. After that year, Father introduced the parish to the practice of the sacraments of Baptism and First Eucharist to be shared with the parish during Mass. We continued this practice because it shared joy the way our oldest daughter received her First Eucharist five years earlier when she was not included in the traditional class.

Like many of us, I learned the word Triduum from Fr. Ron Lewinski. His relentless teaching of the three sacred days has had the biggest impact on me. That first Holy Week, he asked me if he could "wash my feet." I would be in one of the small groups he would wash as he taught the parish about this ritual's meaning. I was about to say no, are you nuts; but the Holy Spirit came over me and I said yes. That Holy Thursday he washed my feet, and I said, "Thank you." His response was "No, thank YOU!" I began to learn what Jesus was teaching that Holy Night! Nearly every year after that, Fr. Ron washed my feet, and I recommitted myself to try to live as a humble servant of Christ. The last time he washed my feet was in 2017 at St Theresa in Palatine where Fr. Ron again was teaching the gift of the Triduum to another part of the flock.

I was often his driver to and from the airport for his many travels to speak in the USA and in many overseas countries. This favor to him was a gift to me, as he would share his stories of the people he would meet and places he traveled to. One time he was concelebrating a daily Mass overseas. I remember him saying it was typical for about 500 people to walk an hour or more to attend daily Mass so they could receive the Eucharist. All his travel stories only deepened my appreciation for the insight he often shared with me. It showed me how well-known he was around the world.

He loved being a priest even during challenging times. He loved what Vatican II brought to the church. I think this was the source of his love for Baptism and the Eucharist. He loved the Liturgy, RCIA, and the Gospels. Being a faithful priest was everything to him. He told me once that teaching our sons by example to love Jesus was the way more men would come to the priesthood. I know his personal example inspired many.

He was a man who lived outside the box. He could take a typical situation and peel it apart with a new perspective that had gone unnoticed.

Relationships were very important to Fr. Ron. He had friends of all ages and backgrounds. I believe he learned something from everyone he encountered. He was an excellent homilist. He would write it on a yellow notepad. And after the last Sunday Mass, I would ask him if I could keep his homily for the purpose of rereading it. He often gave them to me. After a while, he began typing them on his computer and saving them. One of his best homilies was at the funeral of [respected parishioner] Jim McNamara. I still have a copy of it today. I hope someday his homilies are published.

He didn't see himself as a scholar, but anyone who knew him saw he was well read and a was a great writer. He also was not afraid to roll up his sleeves and do physical work. It was a great experience to have him on the mission team to build a house in Belize for two years in a row. He painted, hammered nails, hauled lumber, and led us in beautiful liturgy.

Fr. Ron was a trusting soul. One time he asked me to drive him to the hospital for a medical need that required him to be put under anesthesia. This was a new experience for me in our friendship, so I considered myself just "the driver." As we took the exit ramp off the highway, he said, "By the way, I've never had anesthesia before." Suddenly, I felt the weight of responsibility to keep our pastor of St. Mary's alive and safe from some obscure medical reaction to anesthesia. What do I do if something goes wrong? He registered and sat in the waiting room. Then his name, "Fr. Ron Lewinski" was called. There was a gasp and whispers from two older ladies. "How can he be a priest?! He's not wearing his collar." When I was called to the recovery room, I was nervous and then grateful to see that he survived his ordeal. I was relieved to get him back home. A few days later, I received the most grateful and genuine Thank-You card from him.

Sometimes I was the annoying little sister. I could get away with nagging him when he was stubborn, like when he was unnecessarily hard on himself. He would need some clarity in his perception of a situation. He would listen, be silent, and then take a new approach.

Building the new church was clearly Fr. Ron's calling at St. Mary's. When the time came for more committees, he asked if I would serve on the architectural search team, which I enjoyed very much. He found many little "projects" to keep me involved, too.

When he was designing the font, he had a box of gold tiles he wanted inlaid on the granite floor in the shape of a cross. He needed to give a dimensional pattern of the cross to the tile setter. After we discussed his goal, I constructed a puzzle frame he used to hand select and organize each piece of gold tile that makes up the cross you see on the floor of the font.

He was sure the new church would have vigil candles, but not the typical stand of candle holder from a catalog. He talked to me about how the lights he saw at a particular church reminded him of dancing firefly lights on a beautiful summer night. He showed me pictures and I could see what he saw as he described them. So, when the day came that the black vigil candle holders were anchored to the wall, he asked me to help him be "sporadic and random" in their placement on the wall as everyone's prayers are unique and travel upwards to heaven like the dancing firefly lights.

When Fr. Ron included us in his 25th Anniversary of his ordination celebration in 1997, we saw the love he had for the priesthood and Mundelein Seminary. Soon after the Dedication of the New Church in 2002 he quietly celebrated his 30th Anniversary with his classmates. The parish received a beautiful gift of the wood carving by Andreas Comploj in Ortisei, Italy of the Statues of the Holy Family in the Nativity to be used at our Christmas Celebration.

Fr. Ron had been teaching stewardship near the time of the 33rd Anniversary of his ordination. There was a picture of the Good Shepherd, which was a gift specifically created for him prior to coming to St Mary, that hung in his office. After sharing an idea with a few others, we saw the opportunity to "give back" to him our gratitude in the spirit of stewardship for all that he had given us in planning, building the new church, and growing our parish in honor of his ordination.

The wheels were in motion to create a celebration. I commissioned the artisan in Italy with instructions emphasizing this being a surprise gift in Ron's honor. We included the parishioners by letter and planned a presentation of the Statue of the Good Shepherd to him.[4] It would occur at the end of the 5 pm Mass, followed by food and celebration. I recall his surprise when he came out of the confessional before Mass and saw a larger-than-normal crowd. It truly was a surprise to him that we were able to orchestrate such an endeavor without him "catching on."

Fr. Ron came to us needing our help to build a new church like when Christ came to us as a helpless infant. Then Fr. Ron called us to be mission disciples... to be the Church just as Christ did on Holy Thursday when he washed the feet of his disciples.

We are all called!

Allison recalls a story from her thirtieth birthday: "I wished for a special ring to help dedicate my love for Jesus. My parents bought it for me and gave me a birthday party. Fr. Ron came to the party and gave me and my ring a special blessing. After that, he would call me Sister Mary Allison. The last time I saw him, he said his usual goodbye, telling me to take care of 'these two parents.'"

---

4. A picture of The Good Shepherd wooden statue presented in honor of Fr. Lewinski by the parishioners in 2005 appears near the front of this book.

Gabe Huck

Formally retired
Former Director at Liturgy Training Publications for the Archdiocese of Chicago

From 1977 until 2001 Gabe worked in the Archdiocese of Chicago.

Chicago's fidelity to the Roman Church's much-needed renewal of all dimensions of the liturgy came to life in the Chicago Archdiocese, which became a center for liturgical renewal across the U.S.

Already when Vatican II did its work in the early 1960s, many in Chicago, on all levels, had been prepared over several decades and were ready to bring to their parishes the liturgical vision of the Council. Chicago parishes in the 1960s and early 1970s took on a leadership that shared the insight and renewal for parishes and their members all over the country. What would become Liturgy Training Publications grew from those pre-Council decades and the post-Council leadership the Chicago Church offered to dioceses and churches throughout the United States and beyond.

My part began with phone calls in 1977 from Ron Lewinski. We had become friends a few years before, both of us wanting this liturgical renewal to take hold throughout the parishes. Ron encouraged the Chicago diocesan staff to keep alive their leadership in liturgy—and to enlarge their work. He invited me to meet these leaders in Chicago and apply to take on the periodicals and other publishing. And so it happened!

As LTP began to grow, a staff of two would eventually become a staff of fifty or more. Ron continued his pastoral work , but he was also focusing on what became known as the Rite of Christian Initiation of Adults (RCIA). Through his articles and books (published by LTP) Ron's work would go far beyond the Chicago churches. He helped us start magazines about the RCIA. He was in much demand throughout the US and beyond. The sense Ron had for the importance of this RCIA in the parishes was crucial. And he knew how to spread the news.

In the years Ron served as Director at ODW, he shared his insight and enthusiasm in many ways, including his writing for LTP's publications, always attentive to those next steps parishes needed to take in embracing the need for liturgy as the work of all the people.

Steve Janco

Music and Liturgy Program Director, M.C.M., D. Min.
Friend of Fr. Ron

Well known to many Catholic musicians as a composer, teacher and author, Steve served for ten years as Director of the Rensselaer Program of Church Music and Liturgy at Saint Joseph's College in Rensselaer, Indiana.

In the 1990s, Fr. Ron and I presented a day-long workshop on planning and celebrating the liturgies of the Paschal Triduum. We knew each other well and had worked together on several projects over the years. At that time, neither of us was aware of a published musical setting of the Entrance Song for the Evening Mass of the Lord's Supper. Many parishes were singing "Lift High the Cross" or one of several other hymns. Ron suggested, "Why don't you compose one?" So I wrote a melody for the refrain text and put together a harmonization. My goal was to create a setting that was stately, but not triumphal, given that the Entrance Song on Holy Thursday serves as the opening of the entire Paschal Triduum.

I printed up the refrain and introduced it to the participants at the workshop, saying, "I'm thinking that this is the kind of feel we need to open the Triduum." Feedback was very positive, and a number of participants said, "Write some verses!" I accepted the challenge. Later that year, I put together a composite English translation of the hymn "Pange lingua gloriosi" (Sing, O tongue, the hymn of glory) and used the five stanzas as verses with the refrain. Two years later, "Glory in the Cross" appeared in print.

An important part of Fr. Ron's legacy is that he recognized abilities and potential in young clergy and lay pastoral ministers—and then mentored, supported, and encouraged us. Even better, he respected us as colleagues and invited us to take part in consultations, projects, and other opportunities as they arose.

Ron was a wisdom figure and mentor to me, but our relationship was never teacher and student. Ron provided and pointed me to opportunities for service—and I learned and grew by doing.

Sr. Madge Karecki

Sr. Madge passed into eternity on June 30, 2022
She was an associate of Fr. Lewinski

Sr. Madge Karecki was a Sister of Saint Joseph, Third Order of Saint Francis, with whom she shared her life for 58 years. Sr. Karecki was a former President of St. Augustine College in Johannesburg, S. Africa

During one visit by Ron to South Africa, I took him to a mission where they did weaving. There was a sister there who worked with these women on the gospel stories. Ron had this idea about readings of the scrutinies. [The scrutinies are rites performed on the 3rd, 4th, and 5th Sundays during Lent as part of the Rite of Initiation.] One is the woman at the well, the man born blind, and then Lazarus. Ron wanted to put them above the baptismal font. He asked if they could do something like that. But it was not a big enough place to produce them as quickly as he wanted. There was another place further north. We didn't go there, but he contacted them. I think they sent sketches, and he said yes. So that's how he got the three tapestries of the epiphanies that are at St. Mary's church.

Ron and I became friends because I had been a proofreader for a newsletter about the catechumenate in Chicago. I left in January 1984 to come to Africa. He wrote to me and asked if he could come because he needed to get into a different atmosphere for a while. So I said sure. He was with us for a little over six weeks. That was in 1990; They released Nelson Mandela from prison while he was there. We were glued to the television set, watching history. It was quite a wonderful time to be there.

He did some workshops for me because at that time I was the head of the liturgy office in Johannesburg. He asked me to take him to different places, and I did. Some people were very grateful because he gave workshops. People just loved him. They gave him a Zulu name: "Ithemba Lethu," which means "Our Hope." When you stay among the Zulus, there is always someone with moral authority. They observe you and then they give you a Zulu name.

When I was in Africa, Ron was writing about building the church at St. Mary's. He had studied sacramental theology in Paris. His entire vision was really sacramental. I think that was a very unique quality in someone building a new church: this entire vision of what the church should be in the sacramental rites. When I returned from Africa, he told me what he had in mind. It was a sacramental vision, the powerhouse of the parish.

The Bishop of Johannesburg asked me to do some liturgical education because he wanted to update people. They didn't do the Rite of Election or anything in the Cathedral. I told the Bishop that this isn't a parish rite; it should occur in the Cathedral. So we started having the Rite of Election in the Cathedral in Johannesburg.

Ron was considered very influential with his writing and speaking, workshops, lectures, and other things about the RCIA. It was he who, when the Pope came to Chicago in 1979—John Paul II was having a Mass in Grant Park—Ron got them to incorporate the Rite of Acceptance into RCIA with the Pope presiding. When the Pope arrived, he said to Ron, "I have never done this." The Pope said, "I believe you can teach me the best way to do it." So Ron prepared the Holy Father for the Rite of Acceptance that was celebrated in Grant Park.

Ron was a wonderful personality. He just had such a good sense of humor. You know, he was so good at mimicking accents, he would call me, and sometimes he was a French person, then an Italian person, then the next time Polish, then Spanish. He made me laugh.

Not long before he died, he went to Rome. He was the main celebrant at my Golden Jubilee. During the homily, he was hysterical. He was talking about missions and going to the ends of the earth. He says, "You know, when I was in Africa with Madge, she and I went down to a working gold mine. We had to dress up with hardhats and overalls and boots." Sometimes Ron embellished a little.

One thing that made him even more interesting was his humility. I always found him to be a very wholesome personality. He didn't need to toot his own. He was so convinced of what he was called to do in the Church and in the world, that he didn't have to brag about himself.

He wasn't afraid of other perspectives because he knew that his perspective was so well-grounded.

Fr. John Kartje

Eleventh (current) Rector of the Seminary at the University of St. Mary of the Lake
Seminarian at Mundelein Seminary

Fr. Kartje was ordained in 2002, the same year the new church at St. Mary's parish was dedicated. He earned a BA in Mathematics and a BS in Physics in 1987 from the University of Chicago. In 1995, the University of Chicago's Department of Astronomy and Astrophysics conferred a Ph.D. degree on Fr. Kartje. In addition, he earned a Doctorate in Sacred Theology from the Catholic University of America's Department of Biblical Studies in 2010.

Ron was ordained in 1972. That was perfect timing for implementing the Second Vatican Council. It took a little time for things to filter through. But even before the Council, Chicago was always very progressive. There were English Masses in Chicago before the Council. The one thing I knew about Ron was that his love for the liturgy was profound, so I've got to imagine that he was a real spear-header even at the seminary implementing those changes.

As a student, I had him as an adjunct instructor in 2002. He would come over and teach liturgy. In particular, the course on the sacraments of initiation, his own vision of the vigil and the Triduum, etc. Keleher would have been Rector then, with people going out with a new sense of freedom, going to the parishes, and taking on ministries that would not have been allowed or encouraged before. I think that spirit really carried into the newly ordained priests.

I saw that, during his mid and late career, Ron encouraged seminarians to help. Even after he left St. Mary's and was working with the Archdiocese, he was very involved here in terms of encouraging seminarians to go out and do things in the Archdiocese. He was always giving me feedback, even after I became Rector, based on his interactions with newly ordained priests: what he thought their strengths were and what he thought the seminary could pay more attention to. I'm sure that was very consistent with his attentiveness to his own formation and growth as a newly ordained priest.

As a student here, what we all appreciated about him was his profound knowledge of liturgy. There was no doubt whatever that he knew his stuff. And he wasn't just speaking out of his emotion, though he was a very emotional man in his own way. You could tell he cared deeply about things. The incident in "The Pivotal Pastor" about the purpose and location of the tabernacle is a great example of speaking to someone's passionate feelings but who maybe wasn't so well informed. He taught in much the same way: returning to the sources of Vatican II, taking us back to the early Church Fathers, and what we know about the Rites of Initiation. As you see in the church that the people at St. Mary's collaborated on building, he asked what that concept looks like in a contemporary space. You can't just go back and reconstruct old methods; but how do you keep that very vital movement of the Spirit and be faithful to it so that it isn't just your own personal likes and dislikes? You ask yourself, "What does it look like in a growing suburb of Chicago or the inner city, or wherever?"

One of my strongest memories of Ron was in this very office. In 2017, the Seminary honored him [with the "As Those Who Serve" Award][5] and it was right here that I notified him of that. Just the emotion! He got choked up and quiet and tears welled up in his eyes. It was so powerful and beautiful—his humility and his love for this place and the Archdiocese of Chicago. And he was involved in the universal Church in so many ways.

I have his picture on my desk. There are young seminarians here who he had influenced, and they were really taken aback by his sudden death.

He always had an interest in the future of the Church.

_____

5. The award is bestowed by the University of St. Mary of the Lake. Its honors people, clergy and lay, as admirable representatives of the Church through their lifetimes of service

Bishop Gerald Kicanas

Bishop Emeritus of the Tucson Diocese
Auxiliary Bishop of the Archdiocese of Chicago, Episcopal Vicar for Vicariate I

Bishop Kicanas was ordained to the priesthood on April 27, 1967. He then earned a Doctor of Educational Psychology degree and a Master of Education degree in guidance and counseling from Loyola University Chicago. He was the seventh Director of Mundelein Seminary.

I got to know Fr. Ron through interactions in the Archdiocese of Chicago. I was always impressed by Ron's passion for parish ministry, whether he was an Associate, or studying parishes, or eventually becoming a pastor. So when there was discussion about who might be best to go to St. Mary's, he was certainly the front runner for that as someone who could take what he'd studied and learned and implement it at St. Mary's.

I think the post-Vatican II era was very exciting, especially for those who had gone through the Council and the seminary—which is what Ron and I did. There was a great deal of writing. There was a great deal of talking about how to re-enliven the Church and implement the vision to "open the windows" as it were. So it was an exciting time. For some people, it was also a difficult time. They felt some of the essentials of the Church were lost and somehow we were turning away from the core teachings of the Church, which obviously wasn't true. I think especially about the changes in the liturgy— going to the vernacular, turning the altar toward the people—those were major changes because of Vatican II.

Ron was wholeheartedly embracing the Vatican II documents and trying to help people see their value and the impact they would have on re-envisioning and re-enlivening the Church. I don't think in his mind there was any question about the significance of the documents and his efforts to implement those at St. Mary's.

The environment that Vatican II was talking about was certainly at the forefront of what Ron was thinking when building the church at St. Mary's. He really loved liturgy. That was a big forte of his and something that he felt was a way to form people in the faith. He took a lot of effort to make sure his liturgies were well done and well-prepared.

The success of the project was Ron's determination to see it through. When you build a church, it's not the easiest thing. You have to work with people to develop the design and to raise money. He was a collaborative priest and eager to hear the thoughts of the parishioners, not just to ramrod his own ideas through. I think he did it collaboratively, in a way that resulted in a beautiful space for worship.

He was well read in the USCCB Conference documents. He was very interested in what the Conference put out on parish life or parish ministry because that's what his passion was. So I have every confidence that he would have read "Built of Living Stones," and would have tried to implement it when he was given the responsibility to serve at the parish.

He was very interested in exploring the pieces that make for an effective parish. He visited some parishes that he and Cardinal Bernardin agreed on at the time. This was his interest both as a scholar and as a practitioner. He wanted to identify the factors that create a vibrant, active, and alive parish community.

His work and study were certainly seen by the Archdiocese as something that could be valuable to other parishes. Of course, he worked downtown as well and was trying to implement some insights that he had, and some values that he felt should be part of an alive parish.

Ron was a spiritual man and saw the importance of continuing his own conversion. He was a fan of Thomas Merton. So I think that was partly what attracted him to the Abbey at Gethsemani for some spiritual nourishment. There were a fair number of priests doing that.

In some ways, Ron was a very serious person. He had a good sense of humor as well. I think he was a very mature person, a very focused person, and very intent on what he was trying to accomplish whether it was in his writing or his ministry.

Today, most of the churches that we're building are pretty functional churches; but I think Ron wanted to build a church that would be uplifting, that would be spiritual for people who are praying there, and I think he did a good job on that.

I remember a man who really wanted to follow through and accomplish something good for the Church. A very good man.

Sr. Elaine Marie Klugiewicz

Retired
Second and third grade teacher of Fr. Ron Lewinski

Sr. Elaine Marie Klugiewicz, a Chicago native, was a teacher, and Director of Religious Education and parish minister. She has served at St. Ann, Assumption BVM, St. Michael the Archangel, and St. Patricia, Hickory Hills. She is retired and celebrated her 75th jubilee in 2022.

I can remember Ron Lewinski as a child. Now, this is only 2nd and 3rd grade, and a lot happens through the years.

One thing I recall at the time I taught him is that I was still in traditional garb [nun's habit]. I had a tendency to stand close to the children because my voice doesn't project well and I wanted the kids in back to hear. So I would stand close to the front desk. He was so tiny that he always sat in front. Well, his feet would not touch the floor, so they would swing back and forth and his shoes would bump into my habit—which was my fault for standing that close. I always had to be aware of that.

It was a very large group that he was in, and there was only one class for each grade at Pullman. Ron was supported by his peers. They supported him by including him; he was never pushed aside, never made fun of. He wanted to share things and they would be open to it and accept it. His peers were very cooperative; they didn't make demands of any kind. He was an average student, and a very nice person to work with. Not that he craved attention; but you could see the reaction in him when someone praised his work, the satisfaction that his work was appreciated.

He was cooperative. He was liked by his fellow students. He was kind of on the quiet side, but his peers let him develop according to his own pace, which was a good average. I think he wanted to please people. If they were happy with his work, then he was thrilled about it and made more effort to produce. I felt he would be something someday, but I didn't know what.

Regarding Vatican II, he was one of the first ones that went through the reforms and it was exciting to see that happening. He didn't have the resentment you got from some of the older fellows who thought the reforms were nonsense and that the Church was throwing too much out the window, so to speak. For example, we never considered the communion rail a way to separate people. It was just something of reverence for us, not just an "ordinary thing." So when the rail was removed, a lot of people fought it. I think it was considered something sacred, so there was an education needed about it being taken away.

I was not originally in the RCIA. I decided, "This is new. I better get prepared for it." There was a workshop being given (probably in the late seventies) and he was one of the people giving the workshop —which I didn't know when I enrolled. That's where we reunited. The RCIA wasn't emphasized very much and in some parishes, they did not do it at all. So the workshop is what I thought I needed, not knowing he was conducting it. What he, as the presenter, gave was very nourishing and made it easier for those who attended to not only adjust, but to share it with those they would work with. Which was my case at that time. He did a beautiful job. So, of course, we 'met' there and after that we corresponded yearly at Christmas time, telling stories of what had happened during the year.

During his fortieth anniversary celebration at St. Mary's, in the narthex, they had things displayed and that's where I found a school composition from when he was a little boy. It surprised me that he kept it that long, you know, all those years. But things like that he treasured. That a single piece of paper from all the way back meant so much that he kept it all those years is amazing.

I have to marvel at just hearing the tidbits of what he did throughout his life, especially during his years as a pastor. When I think of this little guy whose feet couldn't touch the floor because he was so tiny.

He knew what it was to be a priest.

Ed & Laura Kuderna

Former parishioners
Participants in the parish expansion

Ed and Laura raised three children at St. Mary's parish. Ed was active in the Men of St. Joseph ministry; Laura was a member of the Communications Committee during the parish expansion.

Fr. Ron was always talking about community; but he was also challenging everyone with "What's our mission, what's our Church's mission?" It had nothing to do with a physical building; it had to do with what our purpose was.

Fr. Ron came in and said, "I want the people to come together as a community." That's when many of these ministries started to evolve and people were actively contributing and taking the lead with it. He wasn't about "check with me" to get it done; he was about validating what direction you're going, then come to the parish for what support you need. He was about clarifying where you're going and then letting people run with those ministries. And adding music was another. That went into the whole design of the church itself.

Ed

Early on, when Fr. Ron started at St. Mary's, he recognized the need to foster the parish's ministries. One of my first experiences was at a gathering of a few men to talk about the future of the men's group. I hadn't been part of the men's group in the past, yet Ron asked me to join. He was so good at calling people by name and offering personal invitations. It did not come easy to him, but he did it. During the session, it became clear that he had a broader and deeper vision for a men's group beyond shooting hoops and talking about the weather. He was interested in nurturing men's relationship with God and one another. That evolved into the Fellowship of St. Joseph, where we explored topics such as why we go to Mass on Sunday, the Beatitudes, and worthiness. Fr. Ron wrote the reflection guides, but also sat with us as a peer. From there, our relationship grew.

Laura

We met Fr. Ron after Mass one Sunday. He approached us with that smile of his and introduced himself. Our lives were never the same after that! Who knew we were going to be called to mission in many different areas of our lives... and a wonderful friendship with him for over twenty years. He definitely had a sense of humor whether it was planning for the new church or laughing with our kids as they swished his church robes or when playing games. He had uncanny sarcasm and wit. The challenge went both ways too, as Ed and our son, Andrew, finagled him into going on a mission in Belize... twice. Those trips were incredible experiences and, along with the little moments spent with him, created memories for a lifetime.

Dirk Lohan

Principal, Lohan Architecture
Architect of the 'new' church at St. Mary's

Dirk Lohan left his native Germany to begin his architectural studies at the Illinois Institute of Technology under the tutelage of his grandfather Mies van der Rohe. After finishing his studies at the Technische Universität in Munich in 1962, he immigrated to the United States and worked closely with Mies on such projects as the New National Gallery in Berlin, the IBM office building in Chicago, and Toronto Dominion Centre. Dirk Lohan is a Fellow of the American Institute of Architects and is registered to practice architecture in the United States and in Germany. Prior to the establishment of his present firm, Lohan Architecture PLLC, Mr. Lohan was the senior principal in Lohan Associates and Lohan Anderson, as well as a principal at Wight & Co. Under his leadership, these firms produced an impressive portfolio of design solutions including such projects as the McDonald's Headquarters Campus, the Shedd Oceanarium, the new Soldier Field Football stadium, as well as many cultural and commercial national and international building projects. Dirk Lohan's architectural designs have won many awards and have been published widely. He lectures regularly on architecture, art, urbanism, and planning, and many of his talks have been published in magazines domestically and internationally.

I was nineteen when I first visited the Farnsworth House. I was starting architecture. Mies van der Rohe was my grandfather. When I grew up in Germany, as a kid and then as a teenager, my room was plastered with pictures of his work. The Farnsworth house was a major piece of his. So I grew up with it. I was familiar with it before I ever saw it. They built it around 1950. I had seen inside and outside pictures of details. It was pretty familiar to me, but being there was an impressive verification of one's imagination.

The idea about building at St. Mary's was to relate to country architecture and architecture in the farmland. I have always believed that every building has its own demands and requirements and should deal with the specifics of that particular purpose. I was very flexible, and I was always interested to study a little and to understand the requirements, in this case, of a Catholic church.

I grew up in southern Germany—Bavaria and other parts of the Black Forest—so there were lots of Catholic churches. I remember playing in one of them, like a small cathedral, but it was a very impressive building. (When I say I "played," it was during the week because they were always open.) I could draw the plan of that church today because it was so impressive to me. I know major Gothic cathedrals and I'm very familiar with Catholic churches in Europe. To be in a building that you found impressive as a child makes you wonder "how can that be done?" [The building] was something that I admired greatly. As a young teenager, I often went to Catholic churches. The priests were a presence in the community.

I went up to St. Mary parish and looked around. I met Fr. Ron, and we hit it off pretty well. We became well acquainted, and I liked him. I think we got along very well with each other. One thing that he and I discussed at length was that this church should not have the linear hierarchical nave where the parishioners sit in rows facing the altar. It was to be more concentric where the altar was the centerpiece of the space.

I approach each project without a preconceived idea. I want to learn. I want to have a dialog. I want the client to express to me what they're looking for. Then I think about the project. One overriding idea that I've pursued all my life is something that was literally from the very beginning in my head. I always want to relate to what I call the 'context.' In other words, where is the building located, what is the neighborhood like, and what are the neighboring buildings? This is called contextual architecture. At the parish, it relates to the Midwestern open landscape. I asked myself what's appropriate; what relates to that; what makes a convincing building? I think you could say that St. Mary's church is that.

It was a good experience and there was an achievable consensus on the direction and design because everybody had a similar thought process. I think I should mention the design process with a client. There are usually brainstorming discussions with a client. Fr. Ron as well as other people were part of that. We met and greeted each other and had a little discussion. He probably asked me if I had any thoughts about the site and location. By that time, I knew what the site was, and the location, the character of the surrounding countryside. So I said, "Well, you're planning to build a church in the middle of country farmland, so maybe it should have a character like a big barn." I said to myself, and then to Ron, how about we make this look like a big barn in the country? Obviously, we give it some refinement and detail so it's not mistaken for a barn; but it fits into the countryside. What occurred to me was the image of a barn standing alone in the field. It is very common, and it came to our minds rather quickly.

He seemed to agree, and I think he was pleased with that notion. Then later, a very important discussion was about how to bring in daylight as a symbol of spiritual light or guidance from above. That's when we devised this kind of light shaft, or spire, that comes out of the roof over the altar. Then there was the smaller chapel on the other side of the wall behind the altar. Altogether, it has the character of a big barn in terms of shape.

There was some discussion of the 'new rules' from the Vatican. It was really that Vatican II had modernized the liturgy and made it more accessible. As a contemporary architect—I'm not a traditionalist—I found him to be very open to new ideas and doing something that didn't rely on earlier approaches to design. He was open, flexible, and accepting of the entire approach—subject to it working within the liturgical guidelines.

Ours was always a positive relationship. I never heard him complain about anything. In fact, I believe he was very pleased with the outcome. As an architect, I design buildings for people all the time. I think one element that persuaded Ron to go with us was that I had a keen sense of giving a building like this not just a good functional layout but also a spiritual quality. I believe very strongly that in architecture—particularly in religious spaces—that there should be something in the space's form and how light is conducted into the building and so on. So that, if you are contemplative, or if you are praying or whatever, there is a mood of spirituality in the building. I can say about myself that when I go to church and sit in the pew, I become contemplative. I reflect upon myself, my life, and my relationships. A lot of what is said in church makes one contemplative and reflects upon what you're doing, so that's what I mean by "contemplative." Inner-directed rather than outer-directed. Daily life is outer-directed. When you go to church, you should reflect upon your inner thoughts. I believe that was important to him.

Something that I had not actually identified before in other churches was the Eucharistic Chapel. It was a brilliant idea of his. The Eucharistic Chapel at St. Mary's is a very beautiful space. And very intimate too, which is nice.

Normally in the churches that I knew, the organ is usually on a balcony at the back, so when they sing you hear it from behind. In one church, though, right next to the altar, all the pipes were exposed. It drew too much attention to itself, away from the central feature. The idea at St. Mary's was to hide it but make it audible.

The beautiful thing about the narthex is that you can expand by putting up folding chairs. I remember that was his suggestion.

I think what made our relationship noticeably different from other clients was the subject of our discussion. I had never dealt with a Catholic church. Another important element was that he needed to get approval from the Archdiocese in downtown Chicago. So did I. They had to approve everything. He was a pretty good diplomat too; or should I say, a salesman of what he wanted to do. But he was a quiet man.

At the church dedication, Cardinal George came up to me and asked, "You're the architect, aren't you? I just want to tell you I love this new church." Of course, I was very proud about that, and I think it is a compliment largely to Ron in many ways.

Deacon John Lucas

Deacon John Lewis passed into eternity on December 21, 2020
John was a Deacon at St. Pat's in Lake Forest and friend of Fr. Ron

Ron was head of the liturgy office in Chicago and he was living at St. Philip's parish in Northfield as a resident. I was active at St. Philip's when I met Ron. We instantly clicked. Partially because of him I became a Deacon in 2000 and Ron was my spiritual director. So we met once a month for four years, and sometimes twice a month as needed.

His insights were always helpful. He didn't preach as much as he tried to help you understand things from his point of view. He'd ask, "Why don't you think about this..." or "Have you tried..." or "My experience is..." It wasn't dictatorial; it was collaborative, and I could tell that he genuinely believed what he was telling me. He wasn't saying it because it was the party line; he was saying it because he believed it and lived it. Through those insights, I got to see really who he was from a different perspective.

Ron and I would go out to dinner once every couple of months. We'd each take five minutes to complain about the Church and then we'd talk about what we wanted to accomplish. We had mutual respect for each other's ability to engage in the life of the Church.

We talked a lot about what it meant to serve the people of the parish. We spent many hours talking about hopes and prayers and the desire to do the right thing that God was asking us to do. He and I connected at many levels, even the stuff that was hard to talk about. We could talk with each other and give each other advice without it being anything other than having respect for each other. I have a huge spot in my heart for him.

He carefully crafted every piece of St. Mary's church from different parts of the world, and he had an explanation for each of them. It is an accumulation of years of his liturgy training. That building was so well researched from California to Italy. There were no bounds on his ability to create that church. If he gave you a tour of that place, he could stop at every station and explain it for twenty minutes. He could explain every piece. It is truly a reflection of who he was.

To me, expanding the parish was a beautiful example of how

inclusive he was of everybody in everything. It showed his openness of mind and willingness to listen to people and to include everyone, not just a certain segment. I think it said a lot about his own personality. When he would talk to me about it, he just glowed like a moonbeam. He was so proud of everything and the reasoning behind it.

Ron could connect with an awful lot of people at not just a surface level; it was truly heartfelt on his part.

He was open and honest and caring and very faithful. He loved the priesthood. I would say he was a model priest in today's world, and he was a contemporary. Many priests were stuck in the sixties, but he wasn't. He didn't resent Vatican II like so many did. He embraced it and traveled around giving talks on liturgy and looking at different churches.

Ron was very articulate, and he didn't miss any detail. He researched everything. He asked questions. Ron had his own opinions, and it was my impression that he wanted those valued by people in the artistic field or the church field. There were many people he talked to. It was the "training" he'd experienced that created St. Mary's.

He had great respect for his bosses. I call Ron the man for all seasons and the man for all people. He related to everybody. He had a genuine passion for the people at the parish.

When someone criticized him, he took it to heart; and wouldn't be upset but would ask, "is that true?" He took criticism as an opportunity for growth. He taught me that early on.

He was great at giving retreats. I remember asking him, "Why don't you come to the retreat house in Mundelein for a retreat?" and he answered "John, the bishop of Carmel [California] invited me out there to stay in a house on the ocean and all I have to do is give a two-day retreat to the nuns; then I can stay for ten days on my own. Why would I want to go to Mundelein?" So I said, "If I were you, I wouldn't come to Mundelein either."

Renew My Church is now prominent. He did that his whole life in his own way. As I read these documents now about Renew My Church, the emphasis is that everything comes from baptism. And Ron knew that early on, and that's probably what fueled his love for the faith. He embraced change, which was unusual for a lot of priests. He always looked at things from a positive side. We'd laugh together and cry together, but it was always a positive experience. I never left him feeling down. He always rejuvenated me. He had that special gift. Other people would say the same thing about him.

He was so well known all around the country, and when he'd talk about the different places that he visited there was no precociousness. It was, in his mind, to be better at what he was doing and always try to improve and get more knowledge about his craft. There's a phrase that Matthew Kelly has on a daily meditation on Dynamic Catholic. I think the phrase would describe Ron: "We all need people in our lives who raise our standards, remind us of our essential purpose, and challenge us to become the best version of ourselves." I would say that's what Ron did for me.

Ron was such a good man. We really find out the quality of people after they are gone.

Why don't we do this when they're alive?

Bob Lyman

Managing Partner and founder of Sequoia Wealth Management
Parishioner at St. Mary of the Annunciation and Pastoral Council Member for the
    Archdiocese of Chicago

Bob is a graduate of the University of Illinois where he earned a Bachelor of Science degree in Political Science. He and his wife, Jill, raised four children. He is active in his children's schools and the community, serving on the board of nearby Carmel High School.

I was on the vicariate board of thirteen parishes. They report to the Archdiocesan Pastoral Council. There were two of us who went down to those meetings. One month, it would be fifty people from all these different places, and the other month there were eight people who were the leadership. I spent five and one-half years with Cardinal George working on that and seeing everything that took place. It was fascinating; it was an unbelievable formation for me. And then, for six months after George died, it was Cardinal Cupich [*].

I got to see how people saw Ron Lewinski outside of the parish, totally different from how people inside the parish saw him. He was an experienced, successful guy; very well-spoken; took the time to listen; very well thought of. That differed from being at a meeting in the school with the parents who had their own parochial views.

A lot of times, Fr. Ron was a little bashful. People interpreted being bashful as being aloof or something, which was crazy. But they didn't take time to know him. He had a good sense of humor.

The people outside the parish saw him entirely differently. I had seen him speak many times at Archdiocesan events, and he spoke all around the country. Whether it was New York or New Orleans, he was always "Mr. RCIA." That's who he was. Everybody spoke to him with reverence. I was at a meeting with Cardinal George in Chicago, and Fr. Ron had spoken to a thousand-plus people. They were all standing for him, applauding. Cardinal George came out and said, "I just want to say what a great priest—a humble priest—this is what a priest is" and he went on and on about Fr. Ron. I thought, wow, it would be nice for people in our parish to see this. Very few people ever got to see that side of him.

I have a really strong feeling that he would have been great as the Rector at the seminary in a different time and place, but we had such a need for all these guys to be at the parishes.

I've known a lot of parishioners when things were at their worst for them. I had been to funerals where Ron served young children who died. It brought out a side of him that was not the intellectual, philosophical part—it came from his heart. I told him many times that this is the best version of you. It is amazing to see how you are touching people when things are at their worst. Ron was the best when things were at their worst. I think the more you got to know him, you understood that was who he really was. When things are at their worst, you don't forget. That was a side of him that, unless you live through a tragedy, you don't truly understand.

The parish expansion was exceptional. It grew and grew and grew, and all of that was under his leadership. Fr. Ron did not like to ask for money, but that is the reality of what we have to do. We all have different gifts. He gave people the freedom to put their stamp on things. That is unique. Many people like to micromanage.

I remember one time at Parish Council there was an issue about what is the Catholic view on voting. He was always sensitive to keeping religion and politics separate, but there were three or four ministries that wanted to participate. He wanted to make sure that they handled it at one time as a parish. He let people do it, but he wanted it done in structured ways. I thought that was well done.

The other thing I distinctly remember about our church is how we handled the Triduum and how he brought a beautiful tradition and continued for his whole time there—a reverent celebration. That was unique. I haven't had that in other parishes. It continues today; but he did it in a particular way that I had never seen, the washing of the feet and everything else. Really, really well done.

One thing about him as an innovator was that he came up with the concept of combining the three schools because the enrollment is declining—from "no room at the Inn" when my family first arrived at St. Mary's to continue to have building issues and redundancies. He became the guy in the Archdiocese who they came to and asked what should we do differently. He had looked around the country and looked at different places. So he was the founding guy at Frassati Academy for Santa Maria, St. Mary's, and Transfiguration parishes.

Priests coming out of the seminary now are good holy men, but they will not be ready to step up to be pastors when the process is combining parishes together. One might have good ministry; one might have good adult formation. Ron was on the front end of that.

He really was an innovator in so many ways—and again, that speaks to how people saw him from the outside versus from the inside.

Ron would talk regularly about his family. I always thought that those were some of his best homilies, when he shared some of his experiences growing up on the south side and how things were then and living with his family. It was a kind of humble beginning to becoming the father of RCIA and growing the parish. And while we were doing all those things at the parish, he was always serving on committees outside. I saw what many didn't.

From the beginning, I watched how he handled things. He was very comfortable with the kids. I remember he was almost more comfortable with them than with the adults sometimes. But, as a parent, I would watch that interaction. You can't fake things for kids and dogs. They know. If you are phony, the kids or the dogs will pick up on it right away. But he was authentic.

He was certainly reverent. He was an intellectual and lifelong learner. I certainly saw him as somebody who had gifts beyond the parish priest. I saw an intimacy when things were at their worst. Then he was at his best. A shy guy. I thought he was often misunderstood. He was comfortable with other people taking the stage. He wasn't afraid to share the stage, to share responsibility with people. But he was totally comfortable being the leader.

I really think he was a tough critic of himself. I don't think he gave himself credit for things. I said it more than once. You could cut with a knife the difference between how people saw him from inside the parish and the outside. He was very well thought of by Cardinal George, and by everyone in the Archdiocesan office. When I would tell them I was from St. Mary's, they would say, oh we love Fr. Ron. It was unbelievable. Then when you're with the local people, they would be split. I can't believe we're talking about the same guy.

The Men of St. Joseph was a formation for a lot of guys to go through being in small groups. He spent a tremendous amount of time on such things. We have the Lenten missions. He was a prolific writer. I would wonder sometimes when he had the time to do that.

One thing I still look back at today—I was always struck by the time and thought that went into the most minute details of the architecture. The art in the church, the tapestries in the back and how they came from Africa, the statues from Italy, everything had a story. Everything is detailed. I was very struck by all of that. The ceremonial doors—none of that should be taken for granted. How much we had needed the narthex space and how many events have been in that narthex since. That beautiful chapel.

I've spent some of my best times in that Eucharistic chapel. What a beautiful gift. It would have been really easy to just do something different. Many a morning I would sit there early, and I would see everything. It is majestic and simple all in the same place, and it is the perfect place for the King of Kings to be. When you are in there, you are in there with him. It is a sacred, holy place. I knew it didn't happen by accident. I was drinking out of a well that I didn't dig.

I remember when we all walked with Cardinal George at the Pork and Corn Roast to kick off the project. I remember distinctly sitting with Sr. Gael Gensler [*] talking about what we could afford to do. I remember all the meetings that we had through pastoral counsel, planning and development, and the outstanding event to kick it off. I watched the structure go up. I remember how the kids prepared for it at school. Everyone felt like they had a special part. It was very inclusive. I worked the parking lot on dedication day. The dedication was a high holy day. It was pretty special. Everything was well thought out.

In summary, Fr. Ron was seen differently from outside the parish than many saw him from inside. His gifts were on display and his reputation as the author of the RCIA was known far and wide. His intellectual gifts were well suited for the speaking circuit and I attended many a conference where he was one of the keynote speakers. He never disappointed. As for many of us, his responsibilities, personal leadership style, and gifts were a double-edged sword. He was more of an introvert, and many perceived this as disengaged or aloof. My experience was the more I got to know him, the less that this perception was relevant. He surrounded himself with strong leadership in both the school and parish offices.

There was always a transition of leadership within the parish community, but few returned as alumni after their terms as leaders. More than once, I approached Fr. Ron to address this, but he did not enjoy conflict and chose not to address this challenging trend.

Fr. Ron had many associates that had gifts that complemented his own, including Sr. Gael Gensler [*]. Many great initiatives began under Fr. Ron's term as pastor and people felt empowered to share their gifts. St Mary of the Annunciation grew tremendously.

His leadership was critical both inside and outside our parish community.

Anthony Markiewicz

Parishioner at St. Mary's parish
Parish Council and ministry leader

Tony, a dentistry practitioner in Mundelein, and his wife Elizabeth have long been parishioners at St. Mary's parish. They have four children.

I started a Job Ministry at St. Mary's when many people were out of work. Sr. Gael Gensler [*] said, I think you should start a ministry. I said, OK. She walked me over to the office and put a meeting on the calendar before I had time to blink. I did that for about three years.

Ron was completely different from what I had seen in a priest before. He had a vision early on. You knew he was there to build Church. He brought on a lot of really good people. I remember him wanting a pastoral associate, who turned out to be Sr. Gael. He brought in a music director, Jim Scavone [*]. I had never been in a parish before where they actually had a real music director—it was always the widow who played organ on the weekends and a Cantor.

I remember wondering whether he was there to build a church or a community. He was there to build both. But he knew we needed facilities. He knew what he wanted in a church in order to worship properly, and I think sometimes he maybe got a little too "into" the church. I think sometimes he wasn't communicating well enough that he was trying to build community. He really was. He really wanted a community, but you need facilities in order to do it.

I always held him in high regard. He had a very good influence on me and my family. I have never met a priest who tried to form people. He really tried to help you form your faith. I remember one of the first conversations we had. We were sitting and talking and he said tell me about yourself. I said I grew up, I went to Catholic high school, went to Loyola University. We talked, and he said, well you're a dentist, so you have a continuing education. I said, I do. Then he looked at me and said, so when was the last time that you took any kind of course or did any kind of program to help develop your faith? And in a roundabout way, I asked "Am I supposed to do that?" In a nice way, he said, your faith basically stopped forming with your college theology courses. At this point, I was a decade past that. He said, "You need to spend as much time developing your faith as you do developing every other aspect of your life." Over time, he started a number of things and I was able to get involved with those.

What Ron did makes one a better person. It made me much more reflective. It made me more conscious of my spiritual life. It made me more reflective about the choices that I make.

There is a story he shared about Cardinal Bernardin. They had been working on a program, or whatever the doctrinal changes were, for developmentally disabled individuals to receive the Eucharist. Up to that point, they could not because supposedly such people could not make a conscious decision about what they wanted. Fr. Ron said that the Cardinal thought that was ridiculous. They were trying to work on getting it passed through Rome to be universal in the Church because, in essence, you are discriminating against someone who is developmentally disabled. Ron loved the Eucharist and he could not imagine denying someone the Eucharist whether or not they understood it. He said they worked on it for a long time.

They got on a plane to go to Rome when everything was supposed to be approved. The Cardinal got on the plane after getting a phone call and was told that it was going to be denied; that the Curia had united, and that they would not approve it. So Ron said that the Cardinal told everybody that we are still going to Rome. We are going to have a good trip, and they can do what they want there, but we are going to practice what we have talked about.

So basically you have a Cardinal who said "they" are wrong, and "we" are right. We are going to practice it, and if they tell us we can't, then we will deal with that; but it will be an awfully long time before they tell us we can't, and the rest of the Church will probably catch up to where we are. By the time they figure out what we are doing, they won't be able to tell us that. And that is what happened. This would have been when Ron ran the ODW [1984-1994].

I remember during the project at St. Mary's he built support by holding Town Halls. I was one of the people sponsoring the initial Town Halls. We asked people to come in, to learn what people thought, in essence trying to hear what they had to say. But also because it was a small parish that was growing. A lot of the Town Hall was a guided process to not only hear what people thought but also to expose them to what a parish should be like. There was a lot of educating to do. He knew what needed to be done, and he tried to get everybody to feel like they came up with the idea of what needed to be done. That is quite challenging. He was also under pressure because the parish needed facilities.

Our family went on vacation to Hawaii. The Catholic population in Hawaii is historically very poor. We found a parish near where we were staying, which was an old converted gas station. They immediately recognized us as being from out of town. When they came up, they asked where we came from. They gave us leis. They announced us at the beginning of Mass. They invited us to bring up the gifts. It was like we were celebrities who had come to their church. So after Mass, the priest who had celebrated asked us where we were from and I told him, Mundelein. He said small world because he knew Fr. Keusal [former pastor at St. Mary's]. I asked how. He said that Fr. Keusal was a godsend to them. He was serving parishes in Hawaii that don't have priests because there are not enough priests in poor and destitute areas. He was traveling around Hawaii all the time.

Ron was a Liturgist whose view of Liturgy was very rigid, but I would describe him as a liberal priest. One of his shortcomings was avoiding confrontation. His strength was his team. Jim Scavone and Sr. Gael were great individuals whose strengths were Ron's weaknesses.

I think one reason he had difficulty getting things done in the parish was that he could not comprehend that someone did not love the Eucharist as much as he did. Some of us would tell him that people don't understand. It was an area where there was a gap. He had such a deep love and a deep faith, he could not fathom somebody not having that.

Fr. Ron was very influential in the lives of my family.

Fr. Andrew Matijevic

Associate Pastor, Director of Worship, Holy Name Cathedral, Chicago
Mentee of Fr. Ron

Fr. Andy grew up in Palatine and met Fr. Ron while Ron was a resident at St. Theresa Parish in Palatine. They fostered a unique friendship over the three years from when they met to the day he was called home to God. Fr. Matijevic was ordained a priest in 2021, four years after Fr. Lewinski's death, and one of his first stops as a priest was to his grave to bless him, thank him, pray for him, and ask him for his prayers.

I first met Fr. Ron during Lent, on March 4, 2015. It was the first liturgy planning meeting at St. Theresa parish. I remember distinctly that I was across the table from him with the other priests and the liturgy team.

He opened the meeting by asking us what our favorite part of the Holy Week is and what rituals stick out to us the most. So I just sat there as we went around the table. I was a sophomore at the seminary. I was an outsider in the parish, and I didn't really know if he was expecting me to say anything. So he listens to everyone and then he looks at me and says, "Andy, what is your favorite part?"

My favorite part is during the Easter Vigil when the church is dark and they bring in the light and pass it on to the community and it culminates in the Exultet. He just stared at me with his right hand over his mouth and his other arm across his chest. He had this look like it was a profound moment for someone so young to have.

Then Holy Thursday came, and we had the Mass, and he was the celebrant. After the Mass, he came up to me and said, "You did a very good job; it's hard to believe you're only in your second year of philosophy at St. Joe's. You have a keen sense of liturgy and an understanding of how liturgy should work. You're able to see things before they happen, so you have that gift of anticipation."

So on Holy Saturday, we had our walk-thru, just the two of us, so I would know how things work at St. Theresa. He asked me about my vocation story—when I wanted to be a priest. I told him I wanted to be a priest since I was eight, at my first communion. He thought he felt the call at his first communion. So we just kind of bonded. A few days later, I found out my first communion was the day he was ordained a priest—May 10th—so that just deepened our friendship. Then, two weeks later, Cardinal George died. We were both at the seminarian's and priest's prayer service at Holy Name Cathedral two nights before the Funeral Mass.

At the Funeral Mass of the Cardinal, I was one of the servers, and Fr. Ron was in the procession because he was a Dean at the time. Mass was at 12; so we all had to be ready by 11:30. Ron came up to me and asked "Did you eat before this?" and I said, "No, I have some granola bars in my bag." He asked, "Well, lucky you, share some with the rest of us to help us through this Mass."

He and Cardinal George got along really well. Cardinal George really supported Ron during the initial stages of forming Parish Transformation for the diocese. The Cardinal was supportive of everything that he had done at St. Mary's with the church building and all that. He and Cardinal George were very close in spirit and their thinking of moving the Church into the third millennium.

So fast forward a few more weeks. May comes, and Ron and I sit down and talk. He was very open and very supportive. He really took the time to just listen. His heart was very pastoral. He made me feel comfortable and able to share things I wouldn't share with another priest.

He'd visit from time to time and we'd go out to dinner or just hang out at the rectory. I was sharing my theology papers and asked him to let me know if there were any problems before I finished writing it. He was good about it, and very gentle in making suggestions. Most college students wouldn't use sources that he helped with but would help further my argument or research. He was a teacher. I was learning how to be a better writer. He was very supportive.

The following summer I worked in the Parish Mission and Vitality office. It was just getting started, so we spent half the time at Quigley and half the time at the Meyer Center. We would drive to work together and go to meetings and everything. He had a keen sense of Jesus and the people and what they desire. People want to know who Jesus is. Some priests are more concerned about going backward to pre-Vatican II liturgies and everything. People want to encounter Jesus, and the way to do that as a priest is to be present to them, to listen to them, to help them, and to allow them to see that they have a right as baptized Christians to evangelize other people.

So, as Ron and I continued to get to know each other, I kept learning more about who this man was. At the beginning of our friendship, he said we were kindred spirits and at first I didn't understand what he meant or what that really means, but as the months passed we understood each other very well, and we'd text each other about how the day was going. Sometimes we'd go into a really deep discussion back and forth. Other times, neither of us would respond and a whole new set of issues would arise. But he was always available to talk to.

When I was a senior at Loyola, I took a Buddhism class at the Water Tower campus downtown. At that time, he had a room at the house near the cathedral. So every Tuesday night after class, we would go out to dinner. Half the time we'd talk about what was going on in the diocese because Cardinal Cupich [*] was being elevated to the college of Cardinals, and Renew My Church was getting going. In the second half, we'd talk about hopes and dreams and family life and school—very basic human discussions. I really looked forward to those Tuesday night dinners because it was very real. Ron was just a very real person for me during the years I knew him. He was very pensive in his demeanor and his viewpoint, and his ministry.

Then in December 2016, we went out for pie one night in Palatine and he told me that Fr. Kartje [*] asked him to accept the "As Those Who Serve Award" from Mundelein Seminary. He said, "I don't know if I should accept this or not." I said, "I think you should accept it for the people you've ministered to because you've been a servant for forty-five years in the priesthood now. I think you deserve this and you've worked hard for this. You've dedicated your life to the gospel and the message of Jesus."

So that day came in April when he accepted the award. He was thrilled and overcome by the amount of love and affection that was shown both by people inside and outside the community. He was just very happy.

As I continue to remember him over the years, he was a very humble person. He didn't really talk about what he'd done or what he'd accomplished. Other people, whenever Ron would introduce me to someone, would always say "Ron did this" or "Ron did that." He was a leading scholar in the Rite of Christian Initiation of Adults and he was an expert on the catechumenate.

One thing that I really took from his life and legacy is that as baptized Christians, we have the responsibility to further the mission of Jesus wherever we are. You don't have to be a priest to talk about Jesus or lead others to Jesus. That's one of the many takeaways from him.

Another thing he taught me is that the liturgy is so central to the life of a priest, the life of a believer, and the life of a community. So during the liturgy, while people feel engaged and welcomed and accepted, it is very crucial to the life of a parish because if people don't feel this is their home, then where are they going to go? So over the years, he'd give me books on the liturgy, he'd give me articles to read, and we'd have discussions. We would talk about pastoral ministry and how the world is always changing, but the sacraments remain constant. That Vatican II hasn't been implemented as it should have been, but it was a good thing for the life of the Christian.

I don't know where the Church would be today if it hadn't changed. He and I would have discussions about the seminary and some conservative attitudes. He said that some people have a nostalgia for a Church they never knew. Some seminarians prefer to use the Roman Canon every day because they think that's the oldest Eucharistic prayer that was ever written. In reality, it was the second. He and I would have a lot of discussions about different perceptions of Vatican II. Some people want us to go back; but he understood the priest is meant to be the presence of Jesus, not to be Jesus.

In July 2015, he said we were going to take a pilgrimage up to Champaign, Wisconsin, at Our Lady of Good Help. It was a whole day's trip. Another time we went up to Holy Hill. Those little pilgrimages were very significant because it was just him and I. He didn't take any calls from the office. Often he'd come over to my family when he wasn't going to his sister's house in Indiana. Ron was very pastoral. He was just a real priest. He wasn't afraid to show his anger or frustration about a topic. I felt what you saw was what you got. I think that's what I like to see in an authentic priest: a priest who isn't afraid to show their human side, of showing their emotions when there's an emotional topic to talk about.

His death was very traumatic for me because I was in Mexico when it happened and I talked to him the night before, so when I got the call that he had passed away it was very unexpected and I did not handle it very well for the first few months. But as time went on, as I kept reflecting on his life, I realized he wouldn't want me to be somber, but to celebrate the resurrection and that as a baptized person we don't die, because in our baptism we die with Christ and rise with him.

At Ron's funeral, one priest said to me, "You know, you're the last seminarian to be taught by Fr. Ron as a close associate." I took that very personally, very profoundly. Most of the guys at the seminary don't know who Ron Lewinski was. We recently had a Mundelein celebration, and we were honoring all the past honorees. I found it a very good opportunity to share with my classmates who Ron was.

He was very personable and inviting; a great listener. He was very humorous; he liked to have fun. His one-liners—you don't get them anywhere else.

Today, with the state the Church is in, everyone has a call to holiness. Ron really encouraged that and inspired people to do that. He was one of a kind.

I miss him a lot.

Jon & Sue Matousek

Jon is active in ministries and is a former facilitator for Parish Transformation in the Archdiocese
Sue retired as Director of Religious Education and remains a volunteer at St. Mary's

The Matouseks joined St. Mary's in 1988 and remain active parishioners

Jon

I believe Ron was more than a "typical" pastor because he truly could dream great dreams. He had the ability to think, conceive a vision, and develop an enthusiasm, an excitement, a vigor where people could take it on and go with it. It was not just the normal enthusiasm among the people—not just a "rah-rah" enthusiasm, but a cerebral and solid enthusiasm. It really, really always—I think—was centered and focused beyond the walls of St. Mary. I really believe he never felt constrained by the "wall." Even though he built the grand and magnificent jewel that is St. Mary's, he always thought in the broader context. That's why I think he was beyond just a "parish" pastor. In many respects, he was an emerging saint.

He had a universal church vision, not just a parish vision.

There was another quality of Ron's that was well-suited to the folks at St. Mary. He practiced great patience. He took care to go about things in a calm and patient way. There was nothing ever threatening or overly urgent about his demeanor. He had a patient quality to himself.

I had the pleasure of doing twelve Parish Transformation initiatives at parishes other than St. Mary's. I enjoyed the pastors I worked with. By comparison, Ron stood out. The way he carried himself, the way he approached things. He truly was unique. I would have to say that Ron was a special individual. He had that aura about him. Even when he paused to have some fun, he was breathing different air. Even during those casual times, he was still working on several different things. I think that's a tribute to a great visionary.

Now, did he have flaws? Yes, he wasn't a perfect human. But he generated wonderful enthusiasm. He had a good eye for people who could carry the banner and who would walk through walls. He found a lot of them at St. Mary's. But then he was on to the next vision. He relied on your ability to carry things through. He was not into micro-management. Ron had a wonderful way for you to know that he trusted your ability to do it. So that puts even more charge into helping to develop the vision. You could feel his trust. And because of that, you felt obliged to deliver.

There were some struggles. Ron loved his flock. The demons that emerged were from those who reacted to him in very un-Christian ways. During the Town Hall meetings when Ron arrived, there was a shrillness to the opposition against the vision that Ron was sharing. They wanted to keep the "status quo." Ron took it very personally. He became frustrated with some of the leaders in a very personal way. He got very discouraged. But he worked his way through it.

Some of that discouragement, after St. Mary's, was because of being in a different environment after eighteen years of being pastor, a shepherd to his flock. It is like an employee going from one company to another. It was a significant transition.

Ron was not an extrovert; he was not a natural "people person." Some people had problems with that, but to do what he did for eighteen years, I think it took daily and fervent prayer on his part. He met and dealt with his own shortcomings and demons, perhaps even on a daily basis. But he still grew St. Mary's and gathered the people. Even while the construction was underway, the parish grew.

Anyone wondering how Ron regarded the presence of the Blessed Sacrament only needed to attend the entire service on Holy Thursday. That's all they needed to do, and it would all come together for them. Like the washing of the feet; Ron took it to a new extent. It went beyond a pastor washing just the feet of the Parish Council members. By engaging the Council and parish leadership to do the washing, and inviting all the congregation to have their feet washed, he triggered something more. It involved both visible and invisible participation. People needed to go through some sort of examination of conscience. They needed to become vulnerable, and motivated enough to step forward and submit to having their feet washed. They needed to acknowledge the act of humility they were witnessing, and derive more value from scripture. That is another way that Ron was something more than a "normal" pastor.

Sue and I observed the conferral of Fr. Ron into the Knights of the Holy Sepulchre while on our parish's Holy Land Pilgrimage to Jerusalem in 2013. I remember being struck with the thought, "This is a very special man."

Over the many years, Ron was our family's pastor, teacher, confessor, celebrant for Sacraments of Baptism, Marriage, Reconciliation, Holy Eucharist, and Anointing of the Sick, parish life builder, co-comic, Parish Transformation director... and older brother I always wanted!

He certainly wasn't perfect, but for so many years, he was always there, in our joys of birth, struggles with life, and pangs of death— Always There, as one might expect of a Very Special Man.

Sue

Our family moved to Mundelein in 1987 and became parishioners of St. Mary's in 1988. At some point, the pastor, Fr. Keusal, recruited me for religious education part-time, I ran a small program of about 100 students who met once a week.

After Fr. Ron became pastor, he hired a music director and a full-time secretary and asked me to manage the Religious Education Program (REP). I was working full-time at Fremont School then but said I could give him time after school hours. He agreed to that. So, for two years, I left Fremont at 3:00 and went to work at the parish.

There were many challenges for Fr. Ron as he focused on building a new church. He hired Sr. Gael Gensler [*] to work with the people while he worked on the building.

Along with the reality of building a big, new church, Fr. Ron knew he needed a smart business person to help him get through this. Mary Hall came on board for that reason.

In 1998, I left my job at Fremont School. Fr. Ron was able to hire me as the full-time Director of Religious Education. During the years of building the new church, the community grew like crazy and the small 100-member REP grew to about 600 very quickly. Changes in class times and dates had to be made, as well as reaching out to a now very diverse community. Fr. Ron was always so supportive of whatever I did, and he mentored me every step of the way.

Many new families moved to the area from all over the country and they brought their ideas, gifts and talents. I don't have to tell you what a visionary Fr. Ron was. Sometimes he saw things differently than the people did. I truly believe he was well respected and loved by many.

I know that I would not be who I am today if he hadn't been such a strong influence in my life.

Chris Needler

Neighbor of Fr. Ron's sister Diane Ciesielski

Mr. Needler is a retired ad agency owner. He also helps people write their life stories.

One summer day, my wife Mary and I were visited by our wonderful neighbors, Richard and Diane Ciesielski [*], and Diane's brother, Fr. Ron.

I really liked Fr. Ron. We hit it off right away. He was intelligent and articulate. I thoroughly enjoyed our conversation. We spoke about the priesthood, touched on some of the St. Mary's story, and learned about Fr. Ron's latest move to the Archdiocese.

Fr. Ron obviously was the right guy for the Archdiocesan job. Everything the Archbishop gave him to do, he excelled at, so he kept getting things to do. That's a testament to the character of the man. I can't imagine Fr. Ron not being successful at anything they tasked him.

He had a great sense of humor. He was very sharp. I had hoped I would get to know him better the next time he came to visit the Ciesielskis, but I never saw Fr. Ron again.

I was shocked when I heard he had died. I miss him.

Kathy Payette

Parishioner of St. Mary's parish

Kathy and her husband Charles raised their two girls and have been active at the parish for many years. Charles often employs his musical skills as part of a small ensemble during the Mass on Holy Days and on special occasions.

Before our kids started attending St. Mary's we were homeschooling, but I would still take the kids to morning Mass. People said, come, this is for everybody, it's not just for the school people. They were so welcoming. Eventually, my kids started going to school there. I remember Ron was making sure that even as home-schoolers; we were welcome.

I loved how he talked to the children during his homilies. He would actually get down from the altar and walk among the students. Whatever the reading was, he would ask a few questions and then he would take some nuggets of what the kids said and form it into a homily. It was just beautiful how he did that. It was something that applied to them, and also the scripture to the adults.

I specifically remember once when he was preaching about the Lord's Prayer: Thy kingdom come, thy will be done. He said, what do you think the "kingdom" is? What kind of kingdom was Jesus talking about? They would raise their hands and say different things. He started to focus on peace, love, and forgiveness. He took those three words that the kids said and he made a beautiful homily that was appropriate for kids about how you can make the world a kingdom of peace—you know, within your families, with schoolmates, with brothers and sisters—and then love, and of course forgiveness. That was just one example of how he could get kids involved and give a beautiful lesson in the homily.

He was so trusting. When my daughter was in the sixth grade, we were interested in starting a Challenge Club for Girls at St. Mary's. It is all over the world. We went in, and Elise did all the talking. She told Fr. Ron about the retreats she went on, the girls she met, and the positive experiences like the prayer card that she got with her prayer. If you're involved in this, you commit to praying a decade of the rosary every day, reading about a saint every day, etc. There are different things they do. She was showing him this, and she had her book of Saints there and was describing her experience.

He said, yes that sounds fine. I just loved how he listened to this sixth-grader and was completely open and trusting that this would be a good thing for our parish. At some point, it fizzled out, but the good news is that there are some people at St. Mary's who are involved with clubs at other locations. So the parishioners are team members elsewhere.

When one of our daughters was in eighth grade, the teacher, Debbie Stoeckel, invited me to go to the retreat with them. The Mass was in the little church and the retreat itself for the eighth graders was in the new rectory. This was when Deacon Andrew Liaugminas [*] was there, who is now Father Andrew. He and Fr. Ron together were unbelievable. So he and Fr. Ron celebrated the Mass together. They invited everyone to come up by the altar during consecration. I had never experienced that before. It was just the most awesome thing. It was really amazing, and I never forgot that.

They sent the right person to St. Mary's. A person who could listen. A shy person is good at listening. I think he was very good at listening. I think he heard what they wanted. Instead of him saying "This is the way it is going to be," he'd listen, and usually say this would be a good thing to do, and he let it get started. When people do that, organically I think it is more meaningful.

I think it was his listening and trusting people and trusting that God was in charge of the whole thing. It's God's parish. When you let that happen, and you're a people person, and a good listener, growth happens. That's my opinion.

Deacon Bob Poletto

Deacon at St. Mary of the Annunciation
Deacon, staff member, and ministry leader

Bob and his wife Sue started the PADS ministry at St. Mary's after Fr. Ron's arrival. They successfully managed it for many years. Bob served in the U.S. Air Force and became a deacon at the suggestion of Fr. Eugene Keusal, the pastor prior to Fr. Lewinski.

Most people thought Fr. Ron was a little uptight. He was such a stickler for liturgical correctness. He wanted it right. Sometimes with Easter practice, it's a little loosey-goosey, but with him, it was not. He knew what to do. He was such an expert in liturgy.

Fr. Gene [Keusal] came into a very small parish in 1983. We got to a point where it had to expand. We had built the addition to the school, but Cardinal Bernardin said that if we didn't get 100 students in that school, we would will have to close it. So Fr. Gene grew it and five years later it was 200 and eventually got to 226. Fr. Gene's accomplishment was growing the school. Fr. Ron's job was to expand with a new church and grow our numbers, which he did.

For five years before Ron arrived, on and off, Sue and I were on the night shift for PADS [then known as Public Action Delivering Shelter] over at Ivanhoe Congregational Church. When Ron came, we asked him about sponsoring PADS and he thought it would be a great idea. He was a great supporter, just like Fr. Jerry, our current pastor. We made it work for a long time.

If people didn't know, they thought Ron was on vacation a lot. But half of those times were people outside the parish asking him to give seminars and things like that. He did work for the Archdiocese. He traveled, conducting seminars and teaching. I think it helped the Archdiocese in a lot of ways.

You knew you had a guy who was at the top of his game, so to speak. He was sought out in the Archdiocese, and around the world even, to come and talk as one of the top liturgists. Ron definitely could write. He wrote different books and manuals.

It amazed me the places where he went to conduct seminars—like Saudi Arabia. He might be a little more known on the RCIA side, but most people thought he was one of the top liturgists, at least in the Archdiocese if not beyond.

Msgr. Pat Pollard

Msgr. Pat Pollard of the Archdiocese of Chicago
Director of Catholic Cemeteries of the Archdiocese of Chicago (1983-2017)

Msgr. Patrick Pollard was a classmate of Fr. Lewinski at the University of St. Mary of the Lake/Mundelein Seminary. He has a Master's degree in sociology from DePaul University.

We were typical high school boys. There was a jock and an academic. Ron could move between both groups very well. He was very involved and accepted into both groups. It was a good high school experience for all of us.

In the 1960s, there was a lot of turmoil for the Church. In 1966, Cardinal Cody removed the longtime rector at the seminary and installed Fr. John Gorman [*] as Rector. John later became one of our ancillary bishops.

So, when we came to the Seminary, all the rules were changing. Previously, all seminarians had to wear cassocks to class. I never wore a cassock to class. Everyone was trying to grasp what Vatican II was calling for.

The Church made some good moves and some mistakes. It was devastating for some priests in the faculty. Ron and I both experienced it. Three of my spiritual directors not only quit the seminary, but left the priesthood. It was a mistake in understanding. We lost a tremendous number of people from the seminary—both students and priests—who did not know how to integrate what the Vatican was saying. It was a time of great turmoil.

Ron, like all of us, would read the documents of Vatican II on the same day the professor was reading them. That's how fresh it was. The Council had closed by the time we got to Mundelein Seminary, but the effects were still prominent and would be with us the rest of our time there.

In 1968, we accepted our Bachelor of Arts in Philosophy and that was the last undergraduate degree issued by the University of St. Mary of the Lake. The University no longer issued bachelor's degrees, only Masters and Doctorates. So we were in the last class to receive a bachelor's degree. Then we had four more years.

John Gorman had a Master's in Psychology. He realized that seminary training was too constrained. So we'd have professors and

Jesuits in for the semester. There was a whole expansion of the academic resources that were available.

If John Gorman hadn't been there, Sr. Agnes Cunningham [*] would never have been invited. Until 1966, there were only priests. John was there from 1966 until 1973. His predecessor would never have allowed a layperson, and certainly not a woman, as an instructor.

Young Ron Lewinski was enamored by what Sr. Agnes was teaching. He was just taken by her sense of academic pursuit. She was a very balanced instructor. She was searching for what the Council was trying to share. Her first course that I remember is the teaching of the Fathers of the Church. Ron never forgot that. Ron would go back and study Ignatius of Antioch and other Fathers, and it would come through later in his writings. For example, taking communion in the hand. He would reflect on the Fathers about how to position your hands. I always remembered that, because I worked with Ron trying to instruct people when starting a communion ministry. That's another outgrowth of the Council which now we take for granted. Back then, it was all being introduced. Sr. Agnes' influence was to go back to the Fathers of the Church to see what they were saying, to reach their basic understanding. Otherwise, it would be lost over time.

Something that Sr. Agnes referred to were the footnotes to the Council documents. In those footnotes, you would find more than just citations of Scripture. I remember Ron had me read Josef Jungmann's "The Mass of the Roman Rite." That was one of the great texts of the time. There were many footnotes, and Ron explored them to great lengths. There were quotations from Augustine, and the Council of Trent, and other ideas that go back and forth. It shows that Vatican II was not just some crazy people ranting in 1963.

Section 48 of the "Constitution of the Liturgy (Sacrosanctum Concilium)" talks about the Church and the Liturgy of the Eucharist. One citation in it is Cyril of Alexandria. I know that's one that Ron read extensively. The thing that Sr. Agnes beat into our heads is that sometimes the footnotes have more important information than the text they refer to. I think it is one of the key messages that he certainly picked up, so he devoured every footnote.

The Church had the documents from Vatican II, but it had very little understanding of how to apply them. Ron spent a lot of his time teaching us how to apply the documents of the Church.

I remember losing three of our spiritual directors because the turmoil frustrated them. They were in the seminary and reading the documents fresh like the students and wondering what was going to happen next. A couple of the professors told us it's going to take decades for us to understand what the Council has set in motion. Some people wanted it next week. John Cardinal Cody may have voted for it, but he didn't have a full sense of what it meant. People like Ron would go back and realize that some of the impetus for Vatican II began at the turn of the century with some papers by theologians describing the Church differently.

I was cemetery director when the Order of Christian Funerals arose. LTP printed the full text of the Order, and Ron and I sent it out with a letter we had both signed to every parish. There were 375 issued. Ron and I repeated that again when the Roman Missal was edited and LTP was granted permission to print it. They sent that out with a letter. Otherwise, we knew the pastors would not buy one. They would use the old book. In a very real sense, the renewal would never come to their parish until people heard the new word. It was Ron's doing.

I remember walking through the Eucharistic Chapel behind the altar area at St. Mary's. That was a vision of his: if adoration is what you feel you need at the moment, then come back here to pray. In the main church, we pray a different way. And then he created the Narthex for overflow, or hospitality, or functions and other things, all kinds of possibilities.

Ron would not relegate his work to just academic pursuits. He would help, teach at the seminary, and instruct others. He was a great mentor. His mentees are people who were touched by his competency. He wanted to be a parish priest and make it work. He wanted all of his academic knowledge to be put to practical use. Ron would talk with bishops from Germany, and he would talk with the kids in school. That's our Ron.

There are others who are brilliant professors, but they can't get their hearts into parish ministry. Whereas Ron could write a pastoral theological basis for Parish Transformation or a real in-depth look at what a parish should be about. Then he could write about how that could be part of every parish in the Archdiocese, which was a goal of his. The next hour, he could be out at a parishioner's house sitting around the barbecue pit.

I think a strength he had was the ability to relate. I think other priests could read what he wrote, or speak with him, and realize "he's one of us." He had a different way to get the message across. He knew it. He lived it. Ron wanted to get the message across that I am a parish priest at heart. Yes, I've been gifted with theological insight. Yes, I know how to read the ancient Fathers of the Church, and I can stand with academia—like Sr. Agnes—and talk about Cyril of Alexandria. At the same time, Ron could sit down with a Parish Council, or the School Board, or the finance committee—you know, every part of the Church at St. Mary's.

He was one of those good-hearted people.

Janice Powell

Retired
Former President of the Parish Council and member of the Archdiocese Parish Council;
co-chair of Deanery One

Janice and her husband Tom are parishioners at St. Mary's parish.

I had the honor of being the co-chair of the Parish Council when Fr. Ron was appointed to our parish. I welcomed a nervous but eager priest. Not having had a parish of his own before made him vulnerable to wanting to do a tremendous job.

My recollection of Fr. Ron is someone who believed that the laity can take ownership of their faith and their church by letting them take on the responsibility of leading a ministry that they believe in. Our parish at the time lacked outreach programs. We came to Mass and raised money, period.

If anyone thought we needed a Ministry of the Sick, he said do it. A bible study? Start one. Adult education? Organize it. Help the poor? Support the St. Vincent de Paul Society. It should be noted that with his support we became a vibrant parish.

He was confident enough to delegate authority. However; he was always there for advice if needed.

I always felt he was basically shy around people. Except I always felt he cared very much about us, his parishioners.

He asked me to come along with him to show the architect of our new church some ideas of what a church should be for its parishioners. Five of us spent the day traveling to various churches in the diocese. I have to admit it awed me to be a part of that group.

I believe the architect heard us. Our new church is perfect. Fr. Ron truly loved the building, and I believe the building brought peace to Fr. Ron.

Fr. Ronald Raab

Former Pastor at Sacred Heart Church, Colorado Springs, CO.
Staff member of the Office for Divine Worship, Archdiocese of Chicago, 1987-1990

When Fr. Ron was Director of the Office for Divine Worship in Chicago, he hired Fr. Raab for a position in RCIA. Fr. Raab served as a staff member for three years with Fr. Ron as the Director. The two maintained a friendship throughout Lewinski's life. Fr. Raab is active as a retreat director, blogger, award-winning author, and visual artist.

I was living in Colorado Springs at the time and there was a retreat center there that was going to be doing a weekend RCIA. It would not be done by the Forum on the Catechumenate. They wanted to do their own program. They invited Ron and Bishop Murphy—formerly of Chicago—and a musician from Oregon Catholic Press. I was just starting summer school at Notre Dame. I actually left summer school to come back there [Colorado] to do the liturgy and environment for that conference.

Since it was my first summer school session, I had no idea how difficult it would be to leave Notre Dame for a week. I was trying to study every second that I could while also being involved with the Conference. I remember leaving for the airport after the Conference thinking, "Oh my gosh. Ron Lewinski must think that I am just horrible at this." I just didn't feel like I was present enough for it because I was so preoccupied with school.

Then a bizarre thing happened. It was at the beginning of June 1987. I was leaving the parish in Colorado and I was being assigned to our parish in Hayward, California. This is honest-to-God's truth. It was the day before I was supposed to leave. Everything was packed. I had all my belongings addressed to California. I was cleaning out the top drawer of my desk as a last-minute thing. The secretary walks in and says "There's a Fr. Ron on the phone and I came looking for you because it sounds very important."

So I answer the phone, and it was Ron. He said, "I'd like to have you come to interview for a job."

I said, "Ron, how did you know I was leaving?"

He said, "I didn't."

I said, "Had you called me tomorrow, I'd be gone already." I was going back to Notre Dame for six weeks of summer school, but all my stuff was going to be shipped the following day to California.

Then he said, "Well, don't do that. If you're coming to Notre Dame anyway, just come interview."

I called my Provincial in the Congregation of Holy Cross and explained what was happening. They said, well, okay, go interview. So I did. Then the position in Hayward was filled. Finally, at the end of summer school, I was called by Chicago and they said I got the job. August 1987 was when I moved there. I think it was Ron's effort to affirm young people in the business. I was about 30 years old, but he was really good with that.

He loved the Church and loved priesthood. He loved also making people aware of their gifts through the power of baptism. I think that's really the core of who he was. As a staff person, he could certainly fret and worry like the rest of us. At the core was a genuine interest in affirming people's baptism, and that's what his whole mission was about. He wanted people to understand that baptism is belonging to God and the Church and is a call and challenge to live a life of service and justice. The mission of the Church depends on people living out the call of their baptismal promises.

I think his connection to baptism had everything to do with Vatican II restoring the dignity of Baptism and getting away from clericalism. He desired every layperson to realize their dignity in the Church and their call to serve from the gifts and talents God gave them.

I think the difficulty he encountered at ODW was basically trying to maintain the "vision" because—especially with a diocese as large as Chicago—there was always push-back in the office. People's opinions vary. People did not always understand the value of Vatican II. Today, it would be a very different place than it was in the 1980s. The push-back that we used to get was we weren't doing this or we weren't doing that. And just people's expectations. It was on every side. There were a lot of clergy who didn't want to change, and then there was reluctance about this "new thing." It was just a lot of different stuff from all different sides.

Ron challenged me to be a professional within the Church in the United States. I think he moved me from being an associate pastor to looking at the Church from a national perspective. In the parish, I am representing a Church that is a national voice, not just a local parish voice. I think there were many aspects to that. I think he helped mentor all of us in that way. The staff was all pretty young. It was just a wonderful perspective: to look at the national Church.

When I left ODW in 1990, I went back to parish life and I thought that I had given up on my professional liturgy. So I was dormant for a few years. I went to Portland and started working with the poor and I started writing. I had never written anything before professionally. Then it all came back again. A lot of what I'd learned from him was reinvigorated again when I started working with the poor, and that helped bridge those connections of liturgy and justice. I wrote nothing until I worked in Portland and since then I've written 300 articles.

I think all of those learnings from Ron were stepping stones for me.

John Riggio

Retired after 35 years at Allstate Insurance Company
Chair of the Planning and Development Commission for the project

John earned an undergraduate degree from Marquette University and a MBA from the University of Illinois in Chicago. He and his wife, Julie, raised four children and are still parishioners at St. Mary's parish.

Ron had great vision. There was resistance. He was getting continually beaten on by the parishioners. His ideas were considered mild insanity back then. The abuse he took was terrible. It was vicious. Nobody understands the pressure he was under. The project was an effort by many people, and those of us involved were fortunate to be involved. It was a once-in-a-lifetime experience.

He was very methodical. Rather than argue, he educated people. He had subtle ways of achieving massive things. He revived the name of the parish. He was so good about going back into history and asking 'What is the name of the parish?' That in itself is a huge thing.

Think about all the artwork that we have. He left no rock unturned.

Ron and I spent two days driving around Illinois and Wisconsin as we were trying to figure out what the new church should look like. More importantly, what are we going to do in the interim? We had only the gym in the school. He insisted we go to a gym up in Wisconsin that was transformed into a church because they were building a new church.

He brought a lot of change to St. Mary's. Music during the liturgy, for example. And when we had meetings, he'd start off with a prayer or music. At first, that made many people uncomfortable because they weren't used to it.

Ron had quite a bit of input into the liturgy, here and nationwide, even worldwide.

Jim & Holly Robinson

Parishioners active in choir, St. Vincent de Paul, and ministries at St. Mary's parish

Holly and Jim have long been parishioners at St. Mary's. Holly was on the Parish Council.

Jim

Holly and I have been in choir since we joined the parish. We know another choir member who talked to Ron toward the end of his term and she told him she was sorry she didn't get to know him better, but she was very shy. He said he felt the same way. Well, she hadn't realized that. If she had known he was shy, she might have made more effort. That may be true of other people. But he was really good during meetings when he would get up to talk about things and became really alive. When you had discussions, feedback, questions, and answers, you got to know him better.

I remember Ron doing youth programs and the Fellowship of St. Joseph, which was open to men of all ages. He offered a balanced program of reading and introspection and prayer—it was very good. A lot of us got to know each other because of that. We would take turns presenting to the others about the lives of the saints. He would have books for us to read; we had homework every time, so it was very good.

A story we heard was that when he was in college or the seminary, he went on a trip to the Appalachians with a Catholic group, but it was a Lutheran minister who was running it. They went into a Catholic church to attend Mass. The priest refused to give communion to that Lutheran minister. Ron felt offended. Ron may have objected if any non-Catholic tried to get communion, but in this case, we think he was offended because this particular person understood the faith and the importance of Communion better than this parish priest did.

Holly

Jim attended Catholic schools from the first to twelfth grade. Then he came away from the church for a while. He and I met and were married in the local Protestant church. We occasionally attended services there, but Jim found it wasn't satisfying enough for him. He decided to go back to the Catholic faith. We didn't need to look very far: Jim's parents had found St. Mary's at Fremont Center and attended there when they visited us. I went to church with Jim and we got remarried there that summer in 1994.

I was going to church at St. Mary's for two years asking "am I going to become Catholic? I don't think so. I'm not going to make that jump." My Protestant heritage seemed to stand in the way. And then in 1996, I saw how wonderful Fr. Ron did the Easter vigil. It was in the little church, so it wasn't as big. There were one or two people joining at that time. Jim and I were in the choir, which had an effect on me too. During the service, I was very moved and I decided I would become Catholic. It happened at next year's Easter Vigil.

When Ron led a group of parishioners on a trip to Israel they had a meeting beforehand to ask why we wanted to go there. I had heard the stories all my life, but during that tour, we went places and they told the stories about what happened at each place. When I came back I was so changed.

I wouldn't be Catholic if it wasn't for Fr. Ron.

James Scavone

Former Director of Music & Liturgy at St. Mary's parish

Jim Scavone worked in Church music for six years after earning a Bachelor of Music in music theory. He had been a member of the Music Staff for the Archdiocese and an instructor for the diocesan Cantor School.

I'll never forget my first interview with Fr. Ron. After a somewhat lengthy conversation, he asked if he could hear me play a hymn on the organ. I played "Alleluia! Sing to Jesus." When I finished, he looked at me and said in a very low-key tone, "Thank you, that was very accurate." Having received that rather underwhelming compliment, I thought I had somehow blown it. When I reminded Ron about that a few years later, he laughed. He didn't remember it, but he told me he thought accuracy was key in leading congregational singing, so he must have truly been impressed.

I've fondly remembered that comment often and how that exchange was the beginning of a relationship that has had a profound effect on my life. Ron was so much more than a boss or pastor to me. I consider him a mentor. I arrived at St. Mary with what I felt were solid musical and liturgical skills, but Ron showed me how to be a true minister. Mostly through example, but sometimes through guiding words, he patiently imparted his knowledge. He shared both his passion and compassion. He taught me how to effectively work with parishioners. And I was eager to learn!

As in any situation, there were definitely some tough times at St. Mary. Thinking back, it was probably during the tough times that Ron's guidance was the most valuable. He was always supportive and gave advice in a gentle way. He never shied away from a difficult situation or decision, which taught me to address problems head-on.

Fr. Ron was an expert liturgist. He was also a fine musician. Given that, it would have been easy for him to "take over" the music and liturgy programs at St. Mary's. But that was not Ron's way. He let me run the programs. He offered advice when asked and always had suggestions, but he never overstepped. Again—a valuable lesson taught through example.

I have used all of what Ron taught me throughout my career, even after I changed career paths. I valued his guidance, support, kindness, and, most of all, his friendship.

Fr. Don Senior

Fr. Senior passed into eternity on November 8, 2022

Fr. Senior was ordained a priest in 1967. He received his doctorate in New Testament studies from the University of Louvain in Belgium in 1972, with advanced studies at Hebrew Union College in Cincinnati and Harvard University. He served as president of the Chicago Theological Union for 23 years. Fr. Don was actively involved in the interreligious dialogue, particularly with the Jewish and Muslim communities. He led many study tours of the Middle East.

I knew Ron as a professional. I knew he was a very knowledgeable liturgist, had done work in the Archdiocese, and was a very well-respected pastor. Then, too, he was President of the Board at ACTA.

He was open-minded and progressive, I would say, in his views. A great priest who was trying to implement Vatican II and have a parish that was vibrant in the liturgy. I thought of him as a very outstanding Chicago priest. He was well-known and respected by his peers. Ron was very amiable in the sense that he listened to what other people had to say. He had his own viewpoints, too.

I know they respected him in other parts of the world. He had German counterparts in liturgy and sometimes one of them would come to one of our meetings at ACTA to hear what was going on about the U.S. Church and so on.

My vantage point was more like a colleague. He was true blue. He was also realistic. Ron wasn't sublimely loyal to the local Church. He realized its problems, and he also knew a lot about the international Church and he was in touch with priests in other dioceses. Ron had a very well-grounded perspective.

He had a lot of energy, that's for sure. He was very active, and he read widely. We would discuss many things. I think being President at ACTA was also a wonderful experience for him in the sense that he enjoyed it and learned a lot from talking to different people. We would get proposals, many from Chicago, but also from across the country and around the world. He interacted with those materials, and personally with the people who received grants. I think it really fit his interests, to have this experience for so long, at this Foundation. It was good having him because he knew things; he knew people, and he had pastoral experience. He could evaluate what grant applicants were proposing.

He was distinguished because the Archbishop gave him several important responsibilities beyond his role as pastor. The man was down to earth. He wasn't a goody-two-shoes or something like that. Ron saw flaws and inconsistencies and wasn't afraid to express them, but he was not in any way bitter or caustic. He was realistically engaged.

He was a capable, smart man who knew what was going on and was trusted by his fellow priests. Renew My Church covers a lot of sensitive ground with the consolidation and so on. I think it is a tribute to him that he received these extra duties and that he was held in high regard by bishops as well as his fellow priests and lay leaders in the diocese.

Dave & Jill Stowe

Founding Partner at Adventus Consulting
Parishioners involved in many ministries as a family

Dave and Jill were married in 1993 and have five children. They arrived at St. Mary's parish during the expansion project, prior to the dedication of the new church.

We never realized how special St. Mary of the Annunciation was to our family until we moved to Connecticut in 2017. The welcoming and warmth from Fr. Ron Lewinski and the St. Mary's community radiated during our first Mass and new member welcoming over coffee and donuts in 2001.

The faith and fellowship we experienced with Fr. Ron and St. Mary's touched every aspect of our family's life. The sacramental celebration of Baptism for our daughters, the First Holy Communion for all our children, and the Confirmation of our sons were true blessings.

While every Catholic church shares in the same sacramental celebrations and family gatherings, how Fr. Ron and St. Mary's shared love provided us with an epiphany of God's unconditional love. When our second daughter, Anna, was born, and we found out she had Down Syndrome, Fr. Ron and the community were very supportive of our situation and welcomed Anna in with open arms. While the birth of any child will bring many blessings and challenges to the mother and father, having a child with special needs can also create doubts and questions for parents and the family. How did this happen? Why would it happen? How will we deal with our child's well-being? While these doubts ultimately work their way out, having a strong supportive faith community, we found, is very important.

As Anna grew, we started experiencing many blessings, which gave us a better understanding of God's unconditional love for us. Fr. Ron introduced us to the Archdiocesan program for people with special needs called SPRED. Over time, we met other parishioners who had children or family members with special needs and understood how St. Mary's and the SPRED program could help our family grow in faith. Fr. Ron worked with us and the parish and school to allow Anna to attend the school part-time, while she also attended the local public school for some of her services. While this was important to us, we soon realized that teachers, students, and their families also saw many benefits to having a child with special needs to be part of the classroom environment. While we knew Anna would not be able to remain at St. Mary's elementary school or even attend Carmel High School, those formative years for her and our family provided a solid foundation for when we moved to Connecticut, shortly before Ron's unfortunate passing in 2017.

We were able to enroll Anna in the St. Catherine Academy in the Bridgeport Diocese. St. Catherine provides students and young adults with special needs with education, life skills development, and local area job placement based on each person's abilities. More importantly, though, each November the bishop celebrates a Mass at St. Catherine's for each student to receive their sacraments—Baptism, Holy Communion and Confirmation. The bishop not only confirmed Anna, but she can lector and participate in the Mass. Her ability to read, speak and proclaim God's word is truly a blessing and one that we know Fr. Ron is celebrating with her from Heaven. He saw Anna as a child of God who could and would take part in His Divine plan.

Dan & Amy Thompson

Dan is currently President of the St. Vincent de Paul at St. Mary's

Dan and Amy Thompson have been parishioners at St. Mary's since 1999. They have been active in the parish and school since joining. Their three children attended St. Mary's School. Dan is a former Parish Council President and Amy is a former School Board member. Both were good friends of Fr. Lewinski.

Fr. Ron was open-minded and humble. And fun. That's a side of him I think people who didn't know him well, didn't know about. He loved to socialize.

I think one benefit, and one disadvantage, was that he had a down-to-earth realness about him. He was never putting on a show, which I think some people like to see from a priest. When Ron delivered his homilies, he was prepared and had a great delivery.

In terms of his personality, when you were talking with him you felt very engaged with him. I think some people who maybe didn't feel close to him was because of how they engaged with him. He wasn't the smiley priest greeting you on the way out of Mass. Actually, he was, but I think there's a difference between knowing him and not knowing him. He was genuine in that way.

I don't know that other priests have as good a way to personally cultivate or infiltrate people's lives through the Church like he did. He also made a point of getting to know our son, Andrew. He actually gave Andrew several books to read. So he was challenging a teenager, to kind of mentor him.

Dan

He was really one of the closest friends I ever had in my life. That was a characteristic as well, that maybe it was a mutual friendship from the beginning. He had a way of not just having you as a friend but also challenging you to grow spiritually. My understanding of him and my appreciation for him grew over time. I think that getting to know him as a person over time helped me realize he was a very sensitive person, very hard on himself, and took things to heart. I don't know that I realized it early on, but I learned also that he was very open to new ideas that people would present.

He turned to me on to Thomas Merton. Somehow, by just asking me what I was interested in, he would make specific recommendations of books like Merton's "The Seven Storey Mountain." I loved it. I know he took an annual retreat at Gethsemani. I wish I could talk to him about it now. Thomas Merton has been around for a long time and some people have never heard of him while in other circles he is the classic Catholic writer.

Another book by Merton was about contemplation. I have a lot of books that Ron recommended or gave me, and some for my son. He was willing to go deeper, but always in a way to apply it practically. I saw that with the Parish Council. I think he realized it is nice to have more people involved and get more people to do more things, but I learned quickly what's the point unless there is a deeper meaning for people. We're all in a relationship with Christ, but I would say he was much deeper than most priests in that sense.

He was very supportive and very encouraging. Many people can have a deep spirituality, but how does that rub off on other people? He was effective in getting people to grow. I feel he had a huge impact on our family's spirituality, and on St. Mary's school. I was on St. Mary's School Board for three years with him. His commitment to that, and Catholic education, was beautiful. It impacted our family and I think it will always impact our family.

Amy

One memory I have of Fr. Ron goes back to when we first moved into the area and were trying to select a school for the kids. We looked at St. Gilbert's [Grayslake] and St. Francis [Lake Zurich] and we sort of landed on St. Mary's. The school was full, and we wanted to get our daughter into kindergarten or first grade.

There was something of note that happened pretty quickly after we got here. My brother and his fiancée lived in the city. In fact, they got married in 2000, so this all happened very quickly after we first moved here in 1999. They were engaged and my sister-in-law wanted to do RCIA, but they were in the middle of moving to the suburbs. I asked Fr. Ron if she could do it at our parish. Talk about first impressions—he did not hesitate. He said, of course, she can. So she went through RCIA at St. Mary's.

I don't remember ever having a negative impression of Ron. That first summer we were invited to a picnic at the Rutledge's. That was the first time we met him. We got to know him through the years. He was a shy, introverted person. That kind of person is more comfortable in a situation like Rutledge's welcoming home, but he was warm and friendly to us right from the start.

We started the "Advent for Women" around 2007. It was a great example of Fr. Ron being open-minded and willing to let us—as parishioners—try new things, and being open to new suggestions.

I was at Mass one Sunday in November, and I was getting anxious, as a woman, about the upcoming holiday season. We had three kids at home, and Dan was traveling a lot. It was a lot to hold down the fort and handle Christmas and also honor Advent for what I wanted it to be in my life. I felt like a kind of failure every year when Christmas came, and I felt I didn't really prepare spiritually for Christmas like I wanted to. I felt I let my family down because I was so busy and worried about wrapping everything and making cookies. I felt I wasn't peaceful and spiritual like God wanted me to be.

So I talked with Fr. Ron and told him how I was feeling. I said I wonder if you could have a special Advent Mass for women to help them get in a more peaceful place, and help them let go of all these pressures that society says you should feel—all the expectations and things that aren't important about the Christmas season. If we help women put that stuff on the back burner and focus on Advent, then that would be a genuine gift to their families for Christmas, helping their families experience Advent and the true meaning of Christmas. He loved the idea, and he said let's do it.

So now every year at the first week of Advent we have an Advent Mass for Women. Fr. Ron did the first one. He jumped in with both feet and had all kinds of great ideas. We do a wine and cheese afterward with the ladies. The women love it. They look forward to it every year, the fellowship of being with other women. That's a great testament to Fr. Ron and the kind of priest he was.

I think he was guarded during some moments. He wasn't super comfortable with what people were going to ask him when they were coming out of church after Mass. I remember him seeming uncomfortable in that circumstance, whereas some priests are super comfortable. He was open to helping you. I don't know how different that was from other priests because I haven't asked other priests to do RCIA or to bury my brother. He was willing to help us any time our family needed something. He was always there for us.

Fr. Bob Tonelli

Retired Pastor of St. John the Evangelist Parish in Streamwood, Illinois
Classmate of Fr. Lewinski

Fr. Tonelli's and Fr. Lewinski's graduating class from Mundelein Seminary celebrated its 50th anniversary in 2022. Fr. Tonelli built St. John's [Streamwood] at about the same time that Fr. Ron built the new church at St. Mary's in Mundelein.

It was by God's guidance, you could say, that I came to know Ron. In college, I tended to be with classmates that I could really relate to, and Ron was one of them. He definitely was a person who was very high intensity, and I was kind of the low-key type. But Ron was already ahead of his time. That's what I noticed about him in class. He had a great interest in liturgy. That was his major interest as we were going to classes. Theology was also part of his background, of course, but he had a great understanding of liturgy.

By the time we got ordained, he was already way ahead of the times with his interest in RCIA. He actually wrote articles about it in the seminary. Ron did a thesis on RCIA when he was in the seminary getting his theology degree. His work was on the RCIA (which, by the way, ended up being in the 1983 code of Canon Law).

The Cardinal allowed Chicago to become the guinea pig for the Vatican to resurrect the RCIA process. The Canon came out in 1983, so we had almost nine years of experience by then. They were analyzing how this was going to play out in the parishes. Whenever we did the Rite of Election in the Cathedral, it just kept getting bigger and bigger—going from one service to three and then five. It was really just astronomical how this blossomed.

Before Vatican II, converts would go to a priest at the rectory and meet once a week for a year and then the priest would let them know when they were ready to be baptized. But now, this became much more elaborate, more involved with people and a process. It is about liturgy and an entire process for those who want to become Catholic. Also, questions arose, like "What do you do with ones who are already baptized and are Protestant; how does one include them in the process because they don't have to be baptized? How do you get them Confirmed?" That became part of the process. Then a third category developed somewhere around 1983, which was "What do we do with Catholics who were baptized but never got Confirmed?" So we have three categories of people. I don't think he would ever have thought it would expand like that. but that's what happened.

Ron was reviving some rites that were from the early Church and that's how he incorporated all this. That's why Ron was very instrumental in the nation to not only bring it back but to create a way of approaching how we were going to deal with welcoming adults into the Church. That was his major work as a priest in his early years.

If it wasn't for Ron, I don't know if we would even be talking about this.

I will say that Vatican II and its documents pointed us in a new direction with liturgy and worship. To the average Catholic, all we did was turn the altar around and replace Latin with the language of the people, but there was much more to Vatican II than that.

During RCIA's initial stages, Ron lectured bishops across the United States about it. He wrote a lot of articles about it. I remember our class really promoted RCIA wherever we went because he was promoting it to our class. We all got educated through him about how to do it. The changes in the Mass had to be explained. He was part of that. He became a great lecturer on liturgy.

The motto by 1972 or 1973 was 'Vatican II will not happen unless you make it happen.' The reason I'm singling out these class years is because they were prepared to make it happen.

The seminary classes from the late 1960s did not know what to do because they were still in the Latin Mass. But we were no longer statutary priests doing liturgical ritual; we were going to be evangelizers. That really got to many of us in the classes from 1972 through 1975. We were all on fire. That's how we trained the laity to become involved in the Church. Before, there was nothing for the laity other than being an altar server. There were ushers, but they were looked upon as collecting money. There were no Eucharistic ministers or lectors. When you look at that whole situation, it really took a lot for us younger men to bring about this change.

And then you have the changes in music. The organ was the only instrument one could use. Eventually, guitars came in and trumpets, and all these other instruments which previously could not be used for liturgical events. Ron and I and others in our class were all part of this change. One of our teachers, Fr. Willard Jabusch, wrote some of the early songs that came from Jewish heritage.

We were doing a lot of adult education in the 1970s about the changes, and liturgy was one of them. We were trying to help people understand what this was all about because some of them were upset because there was no Latin anymore. That's because they didn't understand what this was really all about. The guitar music was not music that the older people adapted to as well as young people. They were used to organ, the Latin Gregorian Masses. They were used to just sitting and kneeling. All they did was watch what went on for an hour and use a missal. After Vatican II, the priest at the altar faces the people and says, "the Lord be with you" and the congregation responds.

Ron Lewinski was part of that. He taught us. He said we have to go out there and do it.

Understand that priests familiar with the Latin Mass had not been trained to face people. They were facing the wall. It was easy to forget that there were people behind you. It almost became a private expression of prayer in front of the tabernacle. That's what it looked like. It was like "your Mass," not the "people's Mass." Once we had to turn around and face the people, they trained us in drama—stage right, stage left, eye contact, and so on. The older priests never had to think about that; they were never trained in this way.

Ron was very instrumental in helping us to be better communicators, and to express ourselves and our spirituality when we prayed in front of people. He was also very instrumental in helping us understand the different parts of the Eucharistic prayer. We had a liturgy teacher, Fr. Jerry Broccolo [*], who influenced us, and Ron promoted what was taught.

At the seminary, there was one summer they selected us to be guinea pigs in a new program called clinical pastoral education. It was the beginning of what eventually became a requirement at the seminary. One had to experience three months at a hospital; this was from the Ecumenical movement. All the hospitals that had this program were primarily Protestant hospitals; they were not Catholic. So having a Catholic student in their program was exciting for them.

So back in 1968, we were the first class from the seminary to be selected over the summer to be at a hospital in the city and go through this program. We lived in an old convent on the expressway that they were going to knock down. There were seven of us altogether: three from our class, three from a class ahead of us, and one from the class behind us. We all became priests except the one behind us. We got to know each other. So that's what happened. We were learning from Ron there too, but he was also learning from us because I was very interested in hospital work. I was more into psychology and pastoral ways of approaching patients, but we were all learning what it was like to be a chaplain.

During his priesthood, Ron didn't change much. He was always an excitable person. He was always high-intensity in anything he did. And he was always a guy ahead of his time. He always wanted to learn more. When the time came, he traveled to Europe to learn more about the design of churches.

Ron was an excellent student. He excelled in Church history as well as liturgy. Ron was pretty good at all subjects. He was excellent in the Bible because you had to know scripture to know Church history. He was excellent in general dogmatic theology.

We were allowed to think, and we were also allowed to be creative. That was not true before Vatican II. Vatican II allowed us to be more expressive. Before that you would be "suspect" if you went outside the norms of what we thought was systematic theology or liturgical norms. You weren't allowed to think independently; you had to follow St. Thomas Aquinas' way of thinking. That's why Vatican II is such an important Council in the history of the Church —far more than Trent.

Trent was important because it hinged on the Reformation and it also got our Church getting its act together about where the Church was going. Then, of course, we got locked into it historically for 400 years. So once you get to Vatican II, that kind of opens the door. (St.) Pope John XXIII said let the bad air go out, let some of the fresh air come in, which meant to let the spirit move us. That's exactly what happened. It was a Reformation within the Church—it is a Reformation within the Church. The second Reformation really came about with Vatican II. We're still going through it.

No basic beliefs were changed by the Council, but it looks that way to some people. There was a period when we did not have adoration, we did not have devotion to Mary. The reason is that we were heavily emphasizing the Eucharist because that was the one thing that had not been emphasized. Now, people understand the Mass better and participate in it, and understand scripture. It was the first-time Scripture was being read to them. A lot of people weren't educated in scripture because all they had been taught was the Catechism. I grew up with a Catechism; if I had not gone to the seminary, I would never have learned more about scripture.

Ron's attitude was more about looking to the future, not the past. That's what made him not just a great priest but a great person. He knew his history; he knew about how to be spiritual.

Sr. Agnes Cunningham [*] was a great teacher. She introduced us to Patristics in our first year of theology. This is what we all benefited from when our class went to theology from philosophy. To make that change, we got all new teachers. Previously, we had teachers who had been in the seminary for thirty-some years. They were teaching an old theology; they weren't teaching anything new. It was all systematic theology from St. Thomas Aquinas. With liturgy, it was from a lot of the liturgical masters before Vatican II. When it came to moral theology the same thing happened. So there was hardly any Scripture. That was one of the weakest points of the seminary back in the late 1960s and early 1970s.

So John Gorman [*] took over the Seminary in December 1966.

He had to be a very understanding person: psychologically, how do you go through a reform movement in the seminary? One thing he did was to dismiss several teachers and bring in new ones. He was also in favor of having women who were qualified to teach as well. So he brought in nuns.

Sr. Agnes Cunningham was one of the first ones. She was knowledgeable in Patrology—which was unheard of, for a woman to have this degree. And sister Mary Peter McGinity taught dogmatic theology.

Then Gorman brought in Scripture scholars from other places in Europe and other teachers in the States. He brought our own diocesan priests who already had credentials in teaching theology. It was quite a mix of people and for the first time we were getting introduced to theology that wasn't necessarily Catholic. We had to be introduced to Protestant theology. Because this was an ecumenical movement, we had to be exposed to other philosophies that were out there.

So our knowledge—knowing what the Catholics were saying versus what the Protestants were saying—helped us understand the good that is in both and what we disagree with. That was the blessing of John Gorman. He knew what to do at the right moment. What led up to this was that we had a rebellion in the seminary that no one knew about. We boycotted classes in April 1967 because we were so fed up with many of our teachers.

I know Ron was interested in Thomas Merton. Sometimes,

Merton would be part of his lectures. Our era was very influenced by Thomas Merton and his books. He died in 1968 and we were reading his books while we were in the seminary. I think that got us interested in monastic history and going to Gethsemani.

Ron and I always believed in going to the retreat at a monastery rather than at a retreat center because we wanted to be alone. When you went to the seminary for a retreat, you ran into too many classmates and had meals together, and so on. We wanted silence, to read books, to reflect, to pray, and to pray with the monks. So that's how I stopped going to the seminary for retreat; I didn't consider a retreat as party time. I think that's what also drew Ron away from going to the seminary retreat house. He ran retreats there later on, but he himself did not go on retreat there.

When you go to Europe, the grand cathedrals did not have a tabernacle in the middle, they had it in a side chapel. The altar is the center of attraction, as it should be. The reason we have tabernacles in the middle is an American thing. When we started our country and they built a church, they would not build a brand-new, grandiose cathedral. They didn't have the money and most were farming communities. So they built these A-frame structures, which were small. They had to have something to honor Joseph and Mary. So they put a side altar on each side of the main altar. The tabernacle ended up in the middle, not off in a separate chapel. There was no place to put it except in the middle. That's what people don't understand: this is an American thing, because of country churches. Those became part of the city churches. In Europe, the tabernacle is never the center of attraction. It is the altar that is the center because of the Eucharist. Unless people travel to Europe and see a side chapel, they don't wake up. Many people came from churches where there was a tabernacle in the middle; that's how they grew up.

Ron was doing the right thing with the Eucharistic Chapel at St. Mary's, even though that chapel is behind the altar and you can't see it. It is a chapel for adoration, as well as daily Mass and small celebrations.

If some would just learn their Church history, they would learn something very important. There is no tabernacle, there is just the altar because that is where the Eucharist is presented. The Word of God is central as well. It is a teaching device showing that the Word of God and the Eucharist are equal in the liturgy.

Going back to RCIA and Ron, one of the primary churches to see in Rome, is St. Clement's. Ron had asked if I had ever seen the Basilica of St. Clement. I responded no, but I've seen others. He said this is one of the minor basilicas, but you should see it. When I saw it I was totally awed. Knowing the RCIA, knowing the liturgy, I said I can't believe I'd missed this church. It is called St. Clement after one of the early Popes, the early martyrs around the 100s. He is the one who talked about Church unity. It really is a unique church; they built it on top of the original, which is a catacomb.

It is about a block away from the Coliseum. It is a very unusual church. People who go into it don't see a tabernacle at all. It is a strange setup. You see an altar, and in the middle of the church are panels that go around in a rectangular shape. There are seating areas that face each other. There is an altar at one end and a lectern at the other. The panels separate those who are baptized and therefore considered full Christians. Those interested in becoming Christian stood on the outside waiting to become part of the inside. I learned so much just seeing this one church. This existed in the 300s just after Constantine. This was one of the first churches built.

And then I thought of Ron; thank God for Ron Lewinski. I would never have understood this if it weren't for him. It all makes sense now. I wish more people knew all this. That is the legacy that is Ron Lewinski, whoever knew him.

One idea that Ron gave me when we were building our new church was to have the parishioners participate in a spiritual way. He said, "Have you thought about having the parishioners come inside and have them write a prayer on the cement before they install the carpet and tile? That's only for them so that they can take ownership." So we did that in March 2002. There was a phenomenal reaction. It was a once-in-a-lifetime experience. I watched these people—children, parents, elderly. I went in at the end of the day and I started reading the prayers. I was so overwhelmed that I was crying. These people let their faith shine through the prayers and they had made it their own. It was Ron's idea.

We moved from the old church to the new one on June 30th at night. We needed an idea about how we could say farewell to the old church. We needed some kind of liturgical gesture. We would do a short service and then march to the new church and then repeat the gesture. The gesture our liturgical director chose was to kiss the altar. I was so overwhelmed by this—800 or 900 people going up to kiss the altar, many of them crying. Then they left the old church and kissed the altar in the new church. It was a phenomenal gesture. We had thought it would take about an hour. The whole thing took three hours. When I gave the homily that night in the new church, I said you will never experience this in your life again; this is your house now. It's almost like something Ron would have said: those who are here tonight have experienced a sacred moment in their lives; tomorrow's congregation will never know what you experienced.

Ron was always excited as a teacher and a preacher. When you think about the influence Ron had on us during the seminary and afterward: he didn't educate us formerly as a teacher in a classroom, but we certainly knew about what he did, and the influence he had on all of us, even after we were ordained, because we were reading some of his writings. That's what got us all going. The rest of us educated ourselves as time went on with other things. But he was a significant influence on the class, without a doubt. And in the Archdiocese. Ron understood how people needed to be educated before they could accept something new.

We have six guys in our class out of twenty-seven who ended up building a church. That's highly unusual; I can't believe that we did that.

I miss Ron Lewinski. St. Mary's parish was blessed to have an excellent pastor.

Victoria Tufano

Senior Editor/Liturgical Consultant, Liturgy Training Publications (LTP)
Editor at LTP

Victoria attended Western Illinois University and earned a Master of Arts (MA) at Notre Dame and a Master of Divinity (MDiv) there as well. She has been a Liturgy Director in the Diocese of Des Moines, IA, and a Pastoral Associate/Director of Liturgy at Ascension Catholic Church in Oak Park, IL.

I had met Ron before he was at the Office for Divine Worship [1984–1994]. He and I did workshops for the North American Forum for the Catechumenate. He was on the first one that I ever did. That was in the mid 1980s. I knew him from a distance. I was a Director of Diocesan Worship until 1990 and I may have met him at one of those meetings. Ron was at an infamous meeting in Colorado where the North American Forum was called into being. Jim Dunning was also there. Jim later became the head of the NA Forum. This would have been around 1981 or 1982. The Forum really was the big energy in the U.S. So those dozen people or so recruited people from around the country.

It is kind of odd. Ron seemed very insecure or unsure. He was always kind of that way. He'd say "Ah, I don't know about this workshop tomorrow. I don't think I'm going to give it." And the person who was in charge would say "Ron!" He'd act doubtful and reluctant, but then he'd be brilliant.

I think that Ron liked to bring out skills in other people. He was very encouraging to me. He respected other people's talents and helped them live them. It's a good leadership habit, priestly or not. That's the sign of a good leader, that you are generous in that way.

Regarding his interest in baptism, he told me that when he was doing his Licentiate it was just before the RCIA came out. He wrote about what the ancient texts said about Christian initiation and what that might look like today. I think he basically had written what was in the RCIA and then realized "Oh, this is what I just did." He had a heart for it before it actually came out. The Rites came out in Latin in 1972, and then in English in 1974. He had really turned on to that even before they released it.

Ron wrote one of the early introductory books to the RCIA that LTP published. Then we published a companion piece, so it became a kind of training manual. Now it has become "Introduction to the Rite of Christian Initiation."

He had a lot of connections in Germany. He'd go to Indonesia and do workshops. He went to a conference in Lyon, France. He had a handful of German bishops come to the U.S., more than once. There was a meeting before he left ODW when he talked about the RCIA while there was a translator. So we would talk back and forth. And we showed them the video "This is the Night " (produced by LTP) which was the first video to show baptism by immersion. The German bishops said, "What the heck is this?" They had also never seen where the priest pours oil.

Ron differed from some other RCIA authors because he took a very pastoral approach to it. He wasn't theoretical about it at all. Ron was on the ground with what should happen in the parish and what we're doing for the people. He was intent on sharing that. He taught that at Mundelein Seminary for a long time. After he left the seminary, there was a period when RCIA wasn't taught at the seminary or many other places. The attitude was "Oh, that belongs to the Director of Religious Education. Let them do it." So there really is a dearth of knowledge among not just the very young clergy, but the clergy who are now becoming bishops, who don't have a strong background in RCIA. Bishops love RCIA because at the Rite of Election everyone shows up. It is a celebration with the community.

In 1979, Ron pushed for having Pope John Paul do the Rite of Acceptance into the Catechumenate. That was mind-blowing. It put RCIA on the national screen. He pushed Cardinal Cody into doing that. It was stunning at the time, and it is still pretty stunning.

Fr. Paul Turner

Pastor of the Cathedral of the Immaculate Conception and Director of the Office of Divine
    Worship for the Diocese of Kansas City-St. Joseph
Co-presenter with the North American Forum on the Catechumenate

Father Turner is an author of a blog and several books, and a lecturer on the Catholic liturgy. He holds a doctorate in sacred theology from Sant' Anselmo in Rome. As pastor of diverse parishes, he spent many years ministering in a state prison, serving a Hispanic and multi-ethnic community, and helping the homeless.

They introduced Ron Lewinski to me as "somebody like me" — somebody who had experience as a priest at a parish and also a special interest in the Rites of Initiation. It was in 1990 in Stockton, California. So even before shaking his hand, people had told me, "Oh, you're going to like Ron Lewinski; you have similar backgrounds." It felt like I had known him even before we met. He was kind of a mentor for me in those early days with the Forum Institutes because he had experience with the Institutes where I did not; he had a few more years of life as a priest where I did not; so he wanted to help me make a connection and help me get up on my feet.

Our relationship just grew and grew. I came to appreciate more and more the gifts that he had, the experience that he had, and the genuine warmth that he shared.

From my work with him, I think his strength would be faith in the gospel because he was anxious to share that with other people. He also had the capability to be a good teacher for those who wanted to follow in the footsteps of Christ. He just wanted to share these things with people and create an environment where learning and discipleship could take place. I think those things were important to him.

I guess two things that come to mind—both related to liturgy— would be the reforms to the Mass and the reforms to the RCIA. Ron certainly absorbed the liturgical renewal into his bones and really understood from within what the liturgy and the Eucharist, in its revision, was accomplishing—especially with the participation of the people.

The RCIA was an unexpected gift from the Council. I think it is one of the most important renewals that came about in terms of the different sacraments that were available. There was really quite a change in the process of adult initiation. It was more complicated, but Ron understood all of that. He got inside it and could share it with people. He could make it simple for folks. I think the liturgical renewal brought about by the Second Vatican Council had a great impact on him.

I think the church he built at St. Mary's is a church that celebrates the values of the Eucharist and of contemporary culture. It incorporated modern architecture and art and tried to incorporate the designs that fit the current times and make them work for the liturgy that was given to us by the Council. Some new constructions have not vested as much into the art and architecture as that one did. So it was both an affirmation of the Council's renewal, and of the environment in which the Church is alive right now. It has brought the best of art and architecture into play.

One humorous memory I have of him was during a liturgical conference in France in 1993. It was an international conference on the catechumenate. We took some vacation time together. We both enjoyed the French countryside; so getting out of the city was very appealing to us because we both had some work we wanted to do. We explored things in the region. The thing that I learned about him, that today I can laugh about, was that he did not know how to drive a stick shift. We rented a car, and I ended up doing all the driving because he didn't know how. It turned out fine; he was always very good company. We were within driving distance of Lyon.

I think it says a lot that, even after years of his work at ODW, he really wanted to go into parish ministry again. That was where his heart was ultimately taking him. So he could blend his theological reflection and his servant's heart, bringing all of that to a parish community. He was probably a more reflective and academic priest than others who do parish ministry, but that was what drew him into the people. So, with all of that, he shouldered a very difficult task by bringing that construction project to life. It required additional skills that no priest wants to have to learn: fundraising and building community in a different way. But he did it because he loved the people, he loved the Church. He thought this was a chance to build a strong foundation for the community there and let the liturgy lead the way.

He was happy to be involved, whether it was parish life, construction of the church, doing workshops, forming Frassati Academy, and the latter things he was doing for the Archdiocese in his life. I think all those things filled him with a quiet sense of satisfaction. He also did some work on the English translation of the RCIA back in 1988. That was something he couldn't have said too publicly because at the time you just did that work quietly, it wasn't supposed to be publicized about who was writing what. But he told me he was involved with some of the adapted rites that got published in the 1988 translation. He and a couple of other people worked on that in Washington, D.C.

His fingerprints on the RCIA remain to this day.

Sr. Corine Walsh

Retired
School principal at Fr. Lewinski's first parish after his ordination

Sr. Corine Walsh is among the Sisters of Charity of the Incarnate Word in San Antonio, Texas.

Ron was a young priest at St. Frances of Rome when I took the position of Principal there. It was his first parish. Monsignor Joseph Howard was the pastor. Ron was fortunate to have him as a fatherly mentor. He allowed Ron to have full rein when it came to implementing some reforms of Vatican II.

Fr. Ron had a passion for the Eucharist and for the Liturgy of the Hours—all prayers of the Church as opposed to private prayer. That love and devotion grew as Fr. Ron moved from parish to parish and eventually to St. Mary's. Perhaps what I appreciated most about Fr. Ron was his own personal devotion to prayer. He lived what he preached and was sustained by prayer and contemplation.

Ron was very much into liturgy from the beginning. He would get so discouraged when people weren't delighted, or buy into whatever it was he was doing. I would try to calm him down and tell him, "You know, Ron, you're young; people are older and accustomed to pre-Vatican II. Give them time to get accustomed to new things. You can't just 'push it down their throats'" etc. He always said that I gave him a good foundation, and a shoulder to cry on. We remained very good friends from the time we met.

He was very creative and very intense. When he started a project or got an idea about something, he couldn't rest until he got it moving. I think what I loved about him was he didn't try to do it on his own. He tried to get others involved. Sometimes it worked, sometimes it didn't.

Ron was not all work. He knew how to have a good time and allowed others to do likewise. He loved to travel and did that frequently, balancing his obligations and delegating when necessary.

He was a loyal and loving priest who worked hard to share his talents with and for the people whom he served. Ron was not afraid to begin new experiments. He started so many things.

Ron's passing left a void in many lives and in his case the "good is not interred with his bones." He was a wonderful guy.

Dan Washburn

Retired CFO for a medical equipment manufacturer
Co-Chair with Ann Steffenhagen of the Capital Campaign Committee during the project
   at St. Mary's

Dan and Sandra Washburn are parents of four children and are long-time parishioners at St. Mary's.

My family moved to the community in 1950. We were one of the first non-German farming people. We were definitely "outsiders" in the parish. At that time, the community at St. Mary's were German farmers who were 1st and 2nd generation parishioners. I went to St. Mary's School, which was taught by nuns in a three-room school. Later, after my marriage to Sandra, we moved back into the area and sent our kids to what had become a much larger St. Mary's School. Many of the smaller farms were being bought by developers and the population of the parish was multiplying.

Meanwhile, I had been involved in forming the first Parish Council, coached girls and boys basketball at the grade school, and chaired the Pork and Corn Roast—a major fundraiser for the parish. Fr. Ron enlisted me to be on the building committee and asked me to approach some descendants of the "founding families" of St Mary's parish. I solicited Ken Behm [*], and Ann (Behm) Steffenhagen, along with two of my classmates for eight years at St Mary School—Mary Ann (Obenauf) Mayer and George Diebold.

Before Ron, we'd have guest homilists; but often they didn't return. Fr. Ron brought in people with good sermons, and he was excellent at giving sermons himself. So that was something different right away. Prior to Fr. Ron's tenure, many visiting priests came in, and then out when they began drawing more parishioners to the Masses that they were preaching compared to the pastor. The other thing was an improvement in the liturgy: Fr. Ron had depth in the liturgy. With Ron, the Mass had some meaning. You'd come out from Mass and say "Oh, that was uplifting." That part, to me, was a great improvement.

I liked Ron. Some people thought he was cold. I never had that feeling myself. He had a shyness about him. But in a comfortable setting, he was quite humorous.

There were some people who opposed the transition to a more

open parish environment. However, Ron wanted all voices to be heard on the committee. In one instance, there was a parishioner whose child I had coached. Ron asked me to ask him to be on a committee. To me, that spoke volumes about the difference between Fr. Ron and other pastors. This parishioner was surprised that he was asked because he wasn't a fan of Ron's. He thought about it for a couple of days, but then said, "I can't do it."

I remember going around to different churches during our early deliberation on the overall structure of the design. One we visited was a very traditional church, and a lot of the people on the committee liked it, but Ron didn't like it. He was very quiet about his feelings with the committee. It wasn't long after that we went down to a southwest suburb of Chicago and saw an abbey that really had an effect on the committee. The building had a stark brick wall behind the altar, framed at the top of the wall, with a large wooden crucifix mounted on the wall. It was pretty moving. I was sitting there thinking, wow, this is absolutely gorgeous. Ron saw me and came over and said, "You like that, don't you?" I know that a lot of the committee, including me, felt uplifted by the serenity of the design.

Soon after that trip, Ron laid out several ideas for the altar and an adjoining backdrop. One design he presented had a similar look as that abbey. That visit provided inspiration for the design and look of our new church.

After all these years, I still feel the serenity of that visit to the abbey when I enter our church.

Todd Williamson

Director of the Office for Divine Worship, Archdiocese of Chicago
Student of the Liturgy

The Office for Divine Worship in Chicago works with Archbishop Cupich to implement the vision of the Constitution on the Sacred Liturgy and all subsequent norms issued for Catholic worship and helps parishes most accurately encounter Christ and receive nourishment through prayer and worship. Ultimately, the Office operates to be a resource for parishes, deaneries and vicariates in all liturgical, ritual and observance matters.

Immediately after the Second Vatican Council, the "Constitution on Sacred Liturgy" was the first document that was produced. It called for the renewal of the whole liturgical life of the Church. It said that every bishop should have a commission or an office to assist him with that. Chicago became a leader. Cardinal Cody immediately established a commission that led to an Office. Fr. Dan Coughlin was the first Director of the Office of Divine Worship. During his tenure, he got Ron to work with the RCIA, which at that time was not even mandatory. Cardinal Cody allowed him to really push and establish it.

Three dioceses—Chicago, Detroit, and Los Angeles—really took off with the renewal of the liturgy and establishment of the catechumenate. That would have been in the late sixties. So Ron got involved with the ODW through the catechumenate and eventually became a kind of director of the catechumenate for the Archdiocese, doing what all the commissions and offices of worship were called to do: help the bishop implement the renewal that was called for by Vatican II.

Others were part of it; it wasn't just Ron and Dan. There was Fr. Bob Oldershaw, Pastor Emeritus of St. Nicholas parish in Evanston, IL. He did a tremendous amount in terms of liturgical music. He was doing music, Ron was doing catechumenate, Dan was doing other things. Liturgy training programs began, which became Liturgy Training Publications.

Dan oversaw the office until 1984, when Ron took over. So Dan had it from the early days around 1972 to 1984; that's still only fifteen years after the renewal really began. So, in terms of helping the bishop implement the renewal, that meant working with all the parishes. ODW was about helping the bishop implement changes, but even more, time and energy went into helping the parishes. That was key in terms of the work of the Office at that time: to help plan Archdiocesan liturgies; to help parishes do everything from forming an RCIA team to implementing good liturgical practices: being a resource. Ron was the one who talked John Paul II into the Rite during the Mass at Grant Park.

After leaving ODW, Fr. Dan became Vicar for Priests. Around 2013, Fr. Ken Simpson—who was then pastor at St. Clement parish and a good friend of Fr. Ron's—had Dan Coughlin, Fr. Ron, Sheila McLaughlin and myself—the four directors of ODW—on a panel at his parish talking about liturgy, history, implementation of the renewal, etc. We were at the panel for about two hours. Ron talked about it this way: Dan's concern, when he was Director, was the "first fervor." He said that by the time he himself got to the office, the concern was raising and training ministers. So it was under Ron that the office started not just training sessions, but putting together programs for extraordinary ministers, ushers, liturgy committees, etc. It wasn't "just" doing work around the Archdiocese.

It was also during Ron's time that an annual Liturgy Conference began. In its later years it was out at Dominican University—a whole weekend that drew 1,300 people from around the Archdiocese. Ron helped people see that liturgical ministry is part of our responsibility. Ron was at the ODW until 1994 and then his Associate Director, Sheila McLaughlin, was appointed. She was the one who hired me.

One thing Ron did after ODW was take a sabbatical—a real sabbatical. It isn't just "time off." You're granted time off, but you apply for it. There are a few guidelines about what can/can't happen during the sabbatical. You have to put together what you're going to do on sabbatical for refreshment, renewal, and continued development. So Ron put it together, and they granted him the sabbatical.

He spent his sabbatical traveling and visiting parishes that were known for good liturgy. His work was to learn about what he had identified and bring that back. His whole purpose was to get profiles of how parishes can have a vibrant liturgical life. It is literally where we are now with Renew My Church here in Chicago. It is no wonder that Cardinal Cupich [*] tapped Fr. Ron to be part of that.

I didn't really meet Ron and work with him until the late nineties when I came into ODW. I was probably a bit intimidated. Before I came to ODW, I was on staff in a parish. Ron had already left ODW. I was in college in Michigan. My work and studies were all about liturgy, so I knew who he was and I knew the history of ODW.

When I was hired, this office was the biggest office of its kind in the country. Ron really directed the Office during the heyday. They use different titles, but every diocese has a commission or an office for liturgy. A lot of times people just refer to it as "the liturgy office." So I'm fairly certain that when I first "met" him, he was calling from St. Mary's, asking for some help with something for the parish. I imagine I was at first star-struck because, for those of us who studied Liturgy, Ron was the "Giant." Early conversations with him were all him calling saying (a) "this is the situation, what resources do you have?" and then (b) always always always "so how's it going?" He kept updated in a non-threatening and very supportive way.

Ron was "knowledgeable." He knew the art of liturgy, the art of pastoring, the art of being a good priest and shepherd. He had an enthusiasm for that and was very approachable, not haughty or superior.

Ron had a "downers" side. He was always hopeful; but it didn't take much to get him to go off on a tangent about "how bad things are," and how "it isn't like it used to be." He would lament that, he would lament often.

St. Mary's had the guy who had walked other parishes and other pastors through the building process. He was the guy who had approved plans. That's been part of ODW's responsibilities: approval of the Office is required for new churches, buildings, and renovations. ODW does reviews for architectural, liturgical, and other aspects. There are requirements and prohibitions. We provide a liturgical consultant; and I know for certain that Ron served in that capacity for some parishes. So Ron would have done that with how many other parishes in the Archdiocese. Then, at St. Mary's, he becomes the one who is building a new church.

"Art and Environment in Catholic Worship" was the U.S. Bishop's guidelines and directives for new and renovated churches. A&E had come out in 1978. It was an outgrowth of Vatican II. They replaced it with "Built of Living Stones" in 2000. The themes of A&E and BLS were things that were very important to Ron: the structure of a Catholic church and how it facilitates the liturgy, and how it is a kind of blueprint for the Christian life in terms of prayer and worship, but also the missionary responsibility of every baptized person. That's why Ron favored Pope Francis. That whole idea of missionary disciples, looking outward and not inward. Cardinal George was very critical of churches and had his own ideas. He would, to me, criticize buildings; but I don't remember him ever criticizing St. Mary's church.

Ron had convictions. When he thought something was right, he would hold on and persevere. And not just with parishioners; but also with archbishops and cardinals.

Renew My Church was his most recent passion. He really believed in this process. Both Parish Transformation and RCIA were key models for the development of Renew My Church. It was a recognition of the part of Cardinal Cupich that Chicago, as great as it is, needs renewal. Ron, and others, responded to that by seeing it through the context of Parish Transformation.

Then Ron took the RCIA and used that as a lens to talk about Renew My Church in a unique and, I think, masterful way.

Jim Wojcik

Jim Wojcik passed into eternity in 2021
Jim was in high school when Fr. Ron was assigned to his first parish after ordination

I was a sophomore in high school when Ron came to St. Frances of Rome in Cicero, IL. I can't think of his early years without thinking of him as a parish Associate. Just the way he was as a priest. The way he celebrated Mass. He was a leader even in his early years. St. Frances was his first assignment. Even though he had some hard times trying to get things across to people, I think just his presence as a priest was a driving force in how he conducted things and got people really wanting to become more involved. I think he had a lot of leadership skills that maybe many people in those early years didn't see.

I think it is interesting because when he first came to St. Frances, he was this young priest who was educated and had traveled the world by then. He had studied abroad. I'm not sure that St. Frances was ready for that. He helped us grow into what Vatican II was all about. I remember talking, ten years after Vatican II, and people were still not used to the changes in the Church. He was this new kind of priest who had experienced different things. I think it was hard for people to understand. But people were able to "come around" and learn a lot from him.

He probably pursued as much as he could beyond the seminary. It is interesting because I often think of the people he was with at St. Frances. In those days, there were lots of people in a rectory; there were people who cooked for the priests, and there were people who cleaned for the priests. There were lots of things going on in rectory life, so each priest had their own kind of job to do. The interesting thing about St. Frances was that Fr. Canary [*]—who had been at St. Frances as a deacon—was influential in getting young priests to come to St. Frances because he knew the pastor, Monsignor Howard.

Msgr. Joseph Howard was an Irish priest who felt that if he had young priests to do things and the people liked them and the people learned from them, then he had less to do. So the Associates like Fr. Ron were the ones who were doing everything. Because the makeup of St. Frances was basically blue-collar workers, I think it took time for people to get engaged with Fr. Ron. Although, there was a group of people who did almost immediately. It was a diverse group of people, and that was good. I think that says a lot about his leadership then, and later on as pastor.

Then there was Thomas Murphy, who was a Rector at Mundelein Seminary and then later on became Bishop in Seattle. He was an associate at St. Frances at the time Fr. Ron was there. Msgr. Canary was there as well. All of them were so different. But for the 50th anniversary of St. Frances, Fr. Murphy and Fr. Lewinski did a renovation of the church. It went from one extreme to the other. It had a communion rail and side altars and a big wooden main altar. All of that was taken out, and the modern kind of liturgical pieces of furniture and artwork were put into the church. People by then, mid- to late-seventies, were very open to that. Before Ron Lewinski, we didn't have a decent organ at St. Frances, and we didn't have a decent choir director. He was effective in raising money for an organ.

The experiences of Holy Week with Ron Lewinski are unbelievable. There was one time when he wanted to be sure that everyone—everyone—was a part of the renewal of baptismal promises. He didn't want people just to be sprinkled with water. He wanted everyone to be a part of that newly blessed water. So, we took these small baking tins and put a fish symbol in their bottom, filled them with water, carted them down the aisle, and then passed them down the pews. The symbolism was incredible.

Or the blessing of the fire. There was a staircase that was used in the auditorium that had about ten stairs and it had a small platform at stage level at the top. We actually made a fire in the parking lot, and he was up on top of the staircase blessing the fire. I think about those early days when it was important to understand the symbolism.

We did these dramatic things with the readings on Saturday. There was one time when we had this great choir director that Ron had found. One of her parents got really sick during Holy Week and was having open heart surgery during Holy Saturday, so she wasn't there. Well, one reading we were doing dramatically was the Abraham reading, and she was the voice of God. So, there was no voice of God. And nobody realized it prior. So, spontaneously, somebody filled in.

There was another time when there was a seminarian at St. Frances. Ron wanted him to read the epistle for Holy Saturday as Paul would have done it, without a script, in the middle of the aisle.

The fellow began, then saw someone he knew in the pews, and he went completely blank. Ron wasn't very happy with the seminarian.

Those were the days when deciding whether it was something dramatic or making a symbol stand out was important because people needed to learn those kinds of things, and Ron understood that. Even if there was a flaw, it was still a very powerful thing. He was serious about liturgy.

When he first came to St. Frances, he tried to get to know people. I remember him coming over for dinner; I remember him going swimming with my youngest brother. We lived in Oak Park and had a public swimming pool. He bought a swim pass and my mother sewed it on his bathing suit for him. Even in the years after he left, there was always this caring for people and wanting to know where people were in their lives. Ron attended my father's funeral; when my mother died, he wrote me this beautiful note; when my youngest brother died he wrote a wonderful note. That's probably why Ron Lewinski was the kind of pastor that he was for St. Mary's: he didn't forget about people; he cared about people that came into his life, all along the way. That was important to him.

The initial shock of finding out that he died was like losing someone in your own family. Vicky Tufano [*] called me at the office at Ascension in Oak Park, and I couldn't believe it. But I went home that day and looked at the Christmas card he wrote me. It was interesting that he wrote about how he was so glad that the connection at St. Frances was so good and that it was a continual thing all those years. I thought about that and wondered: was this a premonition of some kind? The one thing that I really miss at Christmas was getting a card from him, his notes.

I think that without the other experiences, he could not have accomplished what he did at St. Mary. I think there were some difficult times for him at St. Mary, but everything that happened until that time had to have fed into what he did. When you talk about the Church right now...I don't think you can build community, I don't think you can build discipleship, unless there's something that has brought you to a point of doing that. I think you have to have both the difficulties and the challenges.

When you talk about Ron related to RCIA and Baptism, that's what it is all about. Now we're talking about Renew My Church. I sometimes think that the entire parish should go through the RCIA process. I think the people who go through RCIA have a better understanding and a different kind of spirituality. I often think of Ron Lewinski as this young priest—and there are other priests after him who have helped me to be where I am spiritually—that had I not had that experience I probably would be one of those fallen away Catholics at this point.

I was at St. Mary's parish for Ron's fortieth anniversary [2012]. The whole complex amazed me. When I walked in for the funeral in 2017, I was more shocked than I was when I heard he'd died. As much as I thought I was ready to see him in a casket, I don't think I was really ready.

Somebody dying suddenly is shocking; but when you think about Ron Lewinski, his death was the culmination of his life. In God's eyes, his job here was finished. But what he brought to people, what he gave to people, continues. That's exactly what our faith is all about.

You know, most people who die after a long illness are remembered for their long illness. With Ron Lewinski, I think he'll be remembered not for the way he died, but for the way he lived.

Fr. Peter Wojcik

Director of Department of Parish Vitality and Mission.
Friend of Fr. Ron and Co-Director of Department of Parish Vitality and Mission in the Chicago Archdiocese

Fr. Peter leads the Pastoral and Spiritual Renewal strategy at the Archdiocese of Chicago, along with serving as the Pastor of Saint Clement Parish in Chicago.

Fr. Ron was very much a man of the Second Vatican Council and the work it accomplished. He was especially interested in the changes to the liturgy that occurred in the 1960s, although as we know, the Church still has a way to go to implement those changes.

Fr. Ron had a pastoral heart and would spend time in conversation with people—listening and making them feel welcome and important. I don't know how he found time to keep up with so many people. There were a very large number of people that he kept up with, which always impressed me.

He enjoyed being a priest and the work he was doing. Fr. Ron always strove to do a very good job and was a pastoral innovator, which is one thing that differentiated him from a lot of other priests. He wasn't afraid to think outside of the box and he did it brilliantly and successfully.

Fr. Ron admired Thomas Merton, and along with St. Thomas Aquinas, referred to them often. He also appreciated Cardinal Bernardin, and the conversations he had with Cardinal George, especially when he started the early process of revitalizing parishes—an early preparation for what is now Renew My Church. Before anybody else, Ron already had an idea about how to initiate renewal. Now we are doing it; but I think it was in his mind and heart years before we even thought about it at the Archdiocese—he was already doing it. It is also an answer to his prayers in many ways that we are doing it now and he led the way.

Fr. Ron was finishing a book on RCIA and was looking forward to promoting it. Unfortunately, it came out a few months after his death. That was one of the amazing things about Ron: you never knew what he was working on, as he was working on so many important things. He would drive an hour-and-a-half between home and work, and then at night write a book! I don't know how in the world he did it, but it was an absolutely wonderful gift.

He also knew when he was on a roll. I remember one day I was in his office, and he was telling me about somebody interrupting a wedding. He related it with so much humor that I was on the floor laughing. Fr. Ron's fun was also reflected in how he would talk about his fondness for Chinese food and, given his excitement, it soon became a standard fare in the office.

When he talked about his sabbatical, he would reflect on trips to the Holy Land and other travels he enjoyed. When Ron and I went to Rome together for one of the evangelization meetings, we met with the Holy Father, which brought much joy to Ron. He beamed while meeting the Holy Father and was able to have a good conversation with him. At one point, one of the security people standing next to the Pope started pulling Ron aside and the Pope actually pulled Ron back to himself. That brought so much joy to him as he appreciated their conversation and it was so wonderful to see.

Fr. Ron could always respond with humor, though he was very serious about our work. He would say, "You know, Peter, we are like the two evangelizers, Cyril and Methodius." They are two saints who were 9th-century brothers we call "Apostles of the Slavs." I think with Ron's Polish heritage and growing up in Chicago, in some ways he felt he didn't belong, as he didn't know many people with Polish last names in the leadership of the diocese. So, in some ways, I think Ron thought, because he was Polish, that he didn't quite belong. But he witnessed a shift in the Church, so it didn't matter if you were Polish or Latino or Irish or Italian or whatever nationality, you had an equal opportunity to contribute to the work of the Church.

He died as one of the top leaders in the Archdiocese. That really was something that he could say never had happened before and it was something he was very proud of.

Stan Zagula

Manager, Quality Programs - EHS and Quality at CF Industries
Member of the Planning Commission for the St. Mary's expansion

Stan and his wife, Brenda, are parishioners at St. Mary's parish and raised their family there. Stan has a Bachelor of Science in Chemical Engineering and a Master of Science in Environmental Health Engineering from Northwestern University. Brenda is an MPT and owner, president, and lead physical therapist of her own business.

When I first met Fr. Ron, it was after Mass when we introduced ourselves at the back of the church. My first impression was he was kind of intellectual and outspoken. As I got to know him over time, I got to see another side of him. He knew he was introverted, and he worked really hard to communicate with groups. It was a challenge because that wasn't his personality. But he thrived in one-on-one and small group sessions.

He asked me pretty early on about the Men of St. Joseph. It was something that Fr. Ron wanted to initiate, to have some spiritual development format. So we started it with some men at the parish.

The other thing he did after he got to know me, and it wasn't too long, was get me involved with the planning for the project, right from the start.

He was well-grounded in Scripture. His homilies always referenced Scripture. Having lived in Evanston and Wilmette, we still went a lot of times to Northwestern. The priest's homilies there were very progressive. They were addressing the college population; they were short, to the point, and "happy" topics of discussion from a homily standpoint. Fr. Ron dug into the dirt sometimes from an intellectual standpoint. It wasn't fire and brimstone; he dug into the Scripture and tried to relate it to our daily lives. And not in a feel-good way all the time. If there were some real issues we were facing, that's what I think he was very good at.

He wanted to have the RCIA welcome people. People who hadn't yet had the experience of the Catholic faith and the history and culture of the Church—that's what Fr. Ron was always trying to bring in.

As I got to know him, I got to understand his knowledge, and it helped my understanding of my faith. I had been born and raised Catholic all my life and never had that depth of understanding. Fr.

Ron brought that forward in his homilies, in the programs he tried to initiate, in the ministries, and in the small faith groups. He really supported the women's faith groups, and he supported the Men of St. Joseph. Those were things he wanted in the parish.

I have a personal connection story about Fr. Ron. It occurred a couple of weeks after a Pork and Corn Roast in August, during a "thank you" party at a parishioner's home for the volunteers. It was a big crowd. Of course, Fr. Ron was there.

During the event, they pulled a young boy out of the swimming pool. He was unconscious and not breathing. There were calls for help. I stopped playing bag toss and went to the pool. I was trained, and immediately had folks taking action: calling 911, going out front to meet the responders, etc. Russell [a parishioner] was there and helped me (we have had a bond ever since). The boy's lips were blue. He wasn't breathing, but he had a pulse.

As I assessed him on the side of the pool, I looked up and my eyes met Fr. Ron's across the way. At that moment, I knew he was praying. It calmed me. My training kicked in. I cleared the boy and did rescue breathing as trained until he was breathing on his own. Soon EMS was there and took over. The boy was our son's age (5 or 6).

I vividly remember the look from Fr. Ron and the words from Russell ("you got this") that gave me the peace and calm to do what had to be done. The boy fully recovered.

Ron was invited to speak all over the world. Many people didn't realize the benefit that we had in Fr. Ron in terms of the gifts that he had. Everyone has gifts. Fr. Ron had certain gifts, and he really developed those well—very creatively.

The structure of the worship space is so important to the overall experience of attending Mass and coming together for all the activities that a parish comes together for. What happens in that building is important. We have been to a few Masses outside in natural settings that were beautiful in their own way. But from another standpoint, that structure is extremely important. Ron had the tools and gifts to bring people together, to bring ideas together, to bring it "out of the people."

I was a docent when we first opened the church. When I think of all the elements and the detail—the "why" behind everything! Why do we have a walkway in the ambulatory for the stations of the cross? Why do they face inside and not outside? Why are the windows small but still bring in light from the outside? Why is the steeple directly over the altar? Why is the baptismal font like a tomb? Nobody but Fr. Ron would have been able to draw that out of everybody and bring it all together.

We had parishioners who were new, and parishioners who had been there for years. A kind of melting pot came together. He drew that out of everybody and manifested it in the building of the church. Now, having said that, maybe his gifts weren't the best at times. Maybe he didn't always say something the right way, or maybe people didn't always like the staff he brought in. For some people that reflected badly on him. I think Fr. Ron absolutely did the best he could. The best thing that he did was draw everything out of the people—I think that's maybe what differentiates him from other priests. He was always wanting people involved. We had Town Halls; we had surveys—there was plenty of opportunity for input. If someone said they didn't have input, then that was their choice.

Fr. Ron was always afraid to ask for money. He did not want to go out and ask for money.

I remember when the steeple cross was delivered to the old church. At the 5 o'clock Mass, Father had a blessing of that cross. Just beforehand, the Men of St. Joseph carried the cross up to the front of the church by the altar. I was impressed by how big it was, and how heavy it was. This thing was going to be at the top of the 50-foot steeple.

I'm thinking that Fr. Ron was not the typical parish priest, because he could get all those things done. He was not always in his comfort zone, but he made things happen. I think it set him apart from other priests.

I know that some thought of Fr. Ron as an intellectual, not approachable. However if you got to know him and understood his many gifts, you would see how generously he shared those gifts with others. That's all you can really ask of a priest, or a person.

God bless him.

Jack & Linda Zucco

Parishioners at St. Mary of the Annunciation

Jack and Linda Zucco joined the parish in 1996. The parish has repeatedly benefited from Jack's professional photography skills.

The Zucco family was blessed to know Fr. Ron both as pastor and family friend.

We helped put up his Christmas tree a few times and had pizza parties at the rectory. He would come for dinners, family celebrations, and sit around the fire pit and roast marshmallows with us. He even went on a Lake Forest bike ride and beach day with us. The boys celebrated a few of their sacraments with Fr. Ron and were altar boys.

Jack traveled to Austria and Italy with Fr. Ron during the summer of 2000. Fr. Ron planned the full itinerary. He called it "Summer in Tyrol… an expedition in search of art." They visited artists and met with the sculptor who created our Madonna and nativity set. There were also hikes, sites to see, history lessons for Jack, good food, and of course, good red wine. To Jack's surprise, on the flight home, he was given a written quiz on the places and history that they experienced together.

Linda said no more trips for Jack while she was home with the boys. So during the summer of 2002, we met Fr. Ron in Maine. Our family traveled for two weeks but stayed with Fr. Ron for a few nights, both in Ogunquit and Bar Harbor, Maine. We had beach days, went sailing, played mini-golf, went whale watching, ate ice cream every night, watched the sunrise at Cadillac Mountain, and most memorable for the boys was spiking Fr. Ron's hair in the hot tub. A few days later, we met him in North Conway, New Hampshire, where he was spending time writing. The boys thought it was cool to celebrate Mass in a hotel room.

It was during these times with Fr. Ron that we came to know more about Ron Lewinski. He felt very close to us and our boys. We know he felt that way about all his parishioners and children of the parish. We wish everyone could have gotten to know Fr. Ron like we did.

Mike Zygmunt

Lifelong friend of Fr. Ron

Probably around 3rd or 4th grade Ron and I started having more responsibility as altar boys. We'd volunteer ourselves to the more complex rituals like Christmas, Holy Week, Easter, etc. In the Church of the fifties, we had many outdoor events: devotions to Mary, Easter, etc. We got involved in these things; and Ron, being more inquisitive about the liturgy and the whole process, used his skills and personality to make it more meaningful.

He wanted things to be more meaningful for people attending, not limit the ritual and habit of events just because we have done them for the last thousand years.

Ron was careful. He learned how to communicate to try to get changes to occur without pushing buttons that would make people nervous. So, for instance, he would try changing music. We had an organist who was very conservative; he lived a few blocks from us; but he liked his job, so he didn't want to rock the boat. Later, when we got older, we were part of a men's choir that sang at the 11:00 Mass on Sundays. That was our first venture into English hymns at that time.

We had a priest, Fr. Ernest, who may have taught at one of the higher-level schools because he was a good speaker, gave good sermons, and tried to relate the world to the Church. He would take things that were mentioned in the news and try to bring them into Church teaching. He made things interesting, so his Masses were well-attended. We had a Mass in Polish but people were still interested. The younger people could pick up on the world around them.

We were intimidated by the monsignor, who was a cigar smoker, an older fellow, and really really set in his ways. In those days it was legal to have Cuban cigars; you could smell them throughout the rectory. It was like having a great-grandfather. When I look back, it was sad because those are the guys you want to talk with. Ron and I were always the two guys selected to be the altar boys for his Mass. The monsignor was difficult; I'll leave it at that. He drove a Studebaker. I remember because in those days when the new season of cars came out, our group—except Ron—was always interested in what was new. The younger priests would talk with us about things like Bobby Hull and Stan Nakita.

Ron and I would work at the rectory. The rectory didn't have a secretary, so during the afternoons or weekends they wanted someone in the house to answer calls, whatever. On Monday afternoon and evening, we'd sort out the Sunday collection envelopes and tabulate them. Then someone would tabulate who gave what.

Across the street from our church, a little north, was a Russian Orthodox Church, maybe St. Michael's. Ron and I were together a lot, and when he'd walk from his house to church, he'd walk past my house. We had no school bus. After school, if we had time, or after a funeral, we'd go visit different places. So we went to St. Michael's and met the priest who was there. Heavily bearded, he had a cassock and crutch. We looked around the church, which was basically similar to ours, but there were different icons and different ornamentation. We had some difficulty later because somehow the nuns found out what we were doing. How that happened we had no idea.

Remember the teachings at the time, if you went to another church, you'd go to hell and all that? So Ron and I, especially later when we had bikes which increased our range of travel, are looking around at a few Protestant places. As young people, we'd walk in thinking a bolt of lightning would kill us; but nothing happened. We found out we could enter the buildings without getting killed. So we'd go looking around. There's a totally different architecture, they had a more modern style of expression. Ron's eyes were opened with the different use of light and the settings.

Ron would attend different churches that had different habits and liturgy. The resistance he encountered at St. Frances, his first assignment as a priest, was that people didn't want to change per Vatican II. But he tried. He would try to make more sense of what the rituals were doing. We had processions for all kinds of events.

I remember he did long-distance trips to Asia and Indonesia. He went to Indonesia and he couldn't wear his clerical garb. There were very few churches, so they had to meet in people's homes. The Islamic community didn't want Christian images.

Changes were occurring, but rarely were they ever spoken about. Fr. Ernie, who was not part of the diocese, would discuss things, but he was thoughtful. He had reasons for different changes. Then you had old-timers. Before Vatican II, we didn't have a Parish Council; that's a "modern" thing. In those days, the Parish Council was a pastor and a priest. There were some outreach programs, but basically, it was difficult to get past the concept of "We did it this way for a thousand years. Why do we have to change?"

Later, after our education, Ron and I got back together; my background is in anesthesia working with surgeons. At Loyola and working at different hospitals, the old surgeons would say, well we did this for twenty years, why do we have to change? Changes are really hard things to accept, especially when you're a young guy coming out of school feeling on top of the world, and you run into guys who try to stop you at every point.

Ron was a very literate guy; a good speaker. He had a little different vibe on the pulpit. Occasionally he'd bring in politics. He was nice.

At St. Mary's, to have Ron with his liturgical expertise, working with Dirk Lohan [*] having the reputation he had, was a unique situation. It goes back to how Ron attempted to change things back in the old church so that people would have a feeling of what was happening beyond just the ritual of the event. He wanted some direction about the activity and the purpose and to get you involved so that you felt you were part of something. In the old days, some people would bring a prayer book or a rosary and not pay attention during Mass. He disliked the idea that you went to church for an hour and then left. That's not what he was looking for.

It was a difficult task to cause change, and it still is.

In Memoriam

CHRISTMAS LETTER · DECEMBER 2016

[Ed.—this was Fr. Lewinski's final Christmas letter.]

Dear Friends,

Christmas greetings and blessings to you and your family!

This is my third Christmas at St. Theresa in Palatine where I live as a resident priest while engaging in full-time ministry at the Pastoral Center for the Archdiocese of Chicago. Last year at this time I was still managing Parish Transformation, an initiative I created to help our parishes undergo a self-assessment of their communities and creatively plan for the future.

Since then a major Archdiocesan renewal effort, Renew My Church (RMC), was launched by Cardinal Cupich to take in an in-depth look at the state of the whole Archdiocese, our 350+ parishes, our vicariate structures and our Archdiocesan Pastoral Offices. I served on a committee that was charged with assessing our current pastoral resources and recommending how our Archdiocesan Pastoral Offices can better serve our parishes. That only led to being appointed to the soon to be reconstructed Department of Parish Vitality and Mission housed at the Cardinal Meyer Center, 35th at the lake. Fr. Peter Wojcik and I serve as co-Directors of this newly formed department that includes offices for Evangelization, Catechesis, Youth and Young Adult Ministry, Marriage and Family Life, Liturgy, Respect Life, Peace and Justice and other Social Ministries—a total of about 60 pastoral ministers under Fr. Peter's and my leadership. I continue to serve on the RENEW MY CHURCH planning committee, and by the way, I am still involved with Parish Transformation. Did someone say I was supposed to be retiring?

The highlight of 2016 was a trip to Rome in September for a Catechetical celebration in conjunction with the Jubilee Year of Mercy. I had the unexpected privilege of concelebrating Mass with Pope Frances in St. Peter's Square and then an awesome opportunity after Mass to meet him personally.

Another highlight was making a retreat at the Trappist Abbey of Gethsemani Monastery in KY, where the great spiritual writer, Thomas Merton, made his home. I've been going there since I was a seminarian. There's a magnetism to the place that in the earlier years was luring me to sign up (but I didn't know that I could have persevered in making fruitcakes and bourbon fudge).

In October I was invited to Fordham University to offer a keynote address on Christian Initiation for the Archdiocese of New

York. During Lent I led two retreats, one at St. Henry parish in Tulsa, OK and the other at St. Joseph in Wilmette, IL. I also squeezed in some time in 2016 to re-write an old classic, Welcoming the New Catholic, which I authored a long time ago. Liturgy Training Publications will release it soon with other accompanying materials.

The award for the most amusing event of the year goes to a trip to Las Vegas where I attended a wedding as a guest of some dear friends. It was a beautiful affair, but with a delayed start. The wedding planner forgot to arrange for a Minister or Judge to witness the vows. No, I did not, could not, stand in. They are now happily married.

What's in store for 2017?

Participating in the planning stages for Renew My Church will undoubtedly take main stage since the pastoral offices I oversee have a major role to play in supporting our parishes. Outside the Archdiocese I'm looking forward to preaching at the Chrism Mass in the diocese of Helena, MT (April 3) and speaking earlier in the day to the local clergy. I will also be speaking at a pastoral conference for the priests in the diocese of Springfield in Illinois in March. Closer to home I'll lead a Lenten retreat at Our Lady of Mercy Parish in Aurora, Illinois. And in early May I'll have the privilege of speaking in the diocese of Brooklyn at a conference on Christian Initiation. Other venues are still in the making…

I'm working hard but I'm holding onto the "ace card" called retirement which I can play at any time. That takes the pressure off and guarantees the necessary freedom to say "enough" when I think the time is right. While I still have the energy, imagination and a reservoir of pastoral experience, I feel driven to share what I can. While I don't believe I have the energy to ever be pastor again, I do enjoy sharing my experience through collaborative pastoral planning, and mentoring others in the ministry, which provides me with avenues to share my ideas. Nevertheless, I dream now and then about a warm and quiet place to retire--my own little Gethsemani. The older we get the more solitude and quiet time we need to thank God for the multitude of blessings gathered over a lifetime. Be assured that if you are reading this letter, you are included in my litany of Thanksgiving.

With love and gratitude for your support and friendship, Ron.

Obituary*

Chicago, IL (July 24, 2017) – Rev. Ronald John Lewinski passed away unexpectedly on Wednesday, July 19 in the rectory at St. Theresa Parish, Palatine. Rev. Lewinski, the Co-Director of the Department of Parish Vitality and Mission, was 71 years old.

Rev. Lewinski was born in Hammond, Indiana on February 15, 1946. He attended the Assumption B.V.M. Elementary School in Chicago and went on to study at Quigley Preparatory Seminary North. He graduated from the University of St. Mary of the Lake / Mundelein Seminary with Baccalaureate of Arts and Master of Arts degrees. After completing his theological studies at Mundelein Seminary and the Faculté Catholique in Lyon, France, Rev. Lewinski was ordained into the priesthood on May 10, 1972 by John Cardinal Cody, Archbishop of Chicago. Rev. Lewinski celebrated his first Solemn Mass at the Assumption B.V.M. Parish on May 14, 1972.

"In his presence, we always were profoundly struck by his deep devotion to Christ and to his ministry as a priest," said Cardinal Blase J. Cupich, Archbishop of Chicago. "Even when retirement was an option, he never considered it as his dream for the renewal of the Church kept him fully engaged, inspired and dedicated. He was a Chicago man; starting out on the south side, moving north and concluding his ministry at the Pastoral Center. He knew Chicago, loved the city and worked very hard each day to bring Christ to its people. We miss him greatly."

Rev. Lewinski served in the Archdiocese in a number of different roles. He was Assistant Pastor of St. Frances of Rome Parish in Cicero (1972-78), Associate Pastor of St. Hilary Parish on California Avenue (1978), St. Marcelline Parish in Schaumburg (1979-84) and St. Joan of Arc Parish in Evanston (1984-95). Over the years of his ministry, Rev. Lewinski served as Director of the Office for Divine Worship (1984-94), the Director of the Cardinal Stritch Retreat House (1995) and became Pastor of St. Mary's of Annunciation-Fremont Center (1996-2014). He was also the Archbishop's Delegate for the Parish Transformation program (2013-16) before becoming Co-Director of the Department of Parish Vitality and Mission in 2016 along with Rev. Peter Wojcik.

Rev. Wojcik considered Rev. Lewinski a great friend and spiritual father. "He was a trusted mentor, not only to me," said Rev. Wojcik, "but also to many other priests and seminarians. They would come to him often over the last 30 years asking for his prayers and support. His sense of humor and willingness to welcome others with a big smile made a difference in countless lives. He is already profoundly missed."

Rev. Lewinski served on the faculty of University of St. Mary of the Lake/Mundelein Seminary which honored him with the "Those Who Serve" award at the Celebration of Mundelein – An Evening of Tribute on April 20, 2017. Rita A. Thiron, Executive Director of the Federation of Diocesan Liturgical Commissions (FDLC), said he was respected around the world for his expertise in the Liturgy and in the Rite of Christian Initiation of Adults (RCIA). Rev. Lewinski addressed the FDLC at the 2014 National Meeting, reflecting on the pastoral issues raised in a 2014 CARA survey on initiation practices. He is the author of several books on the RCIA, including the "Guide for Sponsors" and his most recent "An Introduction to the RCIA: The Vision of Christian Initiation."

Knowing that Rev. Lewinski had been the second Director for the Office for Divine Worship was always an honor for Todd Williamson, current Director of the Office for Divine Worship. "He loved the Church's liturgy and served it diligently his whole priesthood," said Williamson. "He was convinced of its power to transform the people of God, and he never stopped preaching, teaching, writing and speaking about that." Williamson added that in 1979 Rev. Lewinski talked Pope John Paul II into celebrating the Rite of Acceptance into the Order of the Catechumenate during the Mass in Grant Park when Pope John Paul II visited Chicago.

Rev. Lewinski joked about it in his "As Those Who Serve" award speech: "If someone had told me when I rose from the sanctuary floor on ordination day that I would one day re-found a parish, build a church, start a new school, teach in the seminary, coach a pope – now saint – how to celebrate one of the rites of the RCIA in Grant Park, and travel literally around the world in competition with Saint Paul, I would have said, 'You are absolutely out of your mind!'"

Rev. John Francis Kartje, Rector and President of the University of Saint Mary of the Lake / Mundelein Seminary, remembered Rev. Lewinski as an exemplary model of a parish priest who never shirked from tackling new projects and improving life for others. "In many ways he was also a servant to the entire Archdiocese and the universal Church," said Rev. Kartje, "most recently through his leadership with the Renew My Church program. I will always be grateful for the quiet mentoring and spiritual direction he provided to countless men in their vocational discernment."

But he was also a dreamer. Tim Weiske, Director of Strategic Planning and Implementation, said Rev. Lewinski had a gift for observing something as it was and seeing how it could blossom into something else. "He often told the story of Christ Our Hope Parish in Seattle to encourage people to dream about what could be. The diocese bought an old hotel and transformed the main floor into worship space but then, as part of its mission, turned the hotel rooms into affordable housing."

The people of the Archdiocese of Chicago will always be inspired by Rev. Lewinski's vision: "The daily experiences of ministry have all been grace-filled surprises. I've come to the conviction that we must avoid getting stuck in one paradigm of ministry or one period of history. It's the living, breathing and growing body of Christ that has been entrusted to our care and we must love it in all its diversity."

Rev. Lewinski will lie in state on Tuesday, July 25 from 2 to 9 p.m. at St. Mary of the Annunciation, 22333 W. Erhart Rd., Mundelein. Visitation hours will be 9 to 10:30 a.m. on Wednesday, July 26 at St. Mary of the Annunciation Parish followed by Funeral Mass at 11 a.m. Cardinal Blase J. Cupich will be the main celebrant and Rev. Andrew Liaugminas, Director of Calvert House Newman Center, will be the homilist. Interment will take place at St. Mary of the Annunciation Parish Cemetery.

Rev. Lewinski is survived by his sister, Diane Ciesielski of Ft. Wayne, Indiana.

[Ed: Reprinted with permission from Chicago Catholic, chicagocatholic.com.]

Vigil (Vespers)

July 25, 2017

&

Funeral

July 26, 2017

Paul Ciesielski

Vigil Presentation

Hello everyone, my name is Paul Ciesielski and I am Ron's nephew from Indianapolis.

There's no doubt the positive impact Ron had on the Church, his Church family and the Catholic religion itself, for that matter. Every time we come here or to another church function for Ron we are always amazed at the close relationships he had with everyone. He knew SO many people, and SO many people knew him. It's amazing to hear about the impact Ron had here and about all of his lifelong accomplishments and contributions.

And while we all mourn the loss of Ron, I'd like to celebrate his life and to give you a brief glimpse of what he meant to us as a family.

Affectionately known to us as "UR," short for Uncle Ron, he was a loving son, brother, brother-in-law, cousin, uncle, great uncle, and great great uncle. He always took the time for his family, many times traveling long distances for short periods of time just so he could be with his family.

Now perhaps many of you never realized the advantages of having a priest in your family. FREE weddings, FREE baptisms, and another great bonus, on certain holidays we didn't have to go to church. We celebrated Mass in our home with our personal priest.

A few of our favorite family memories:

For twenty-five years, I gave UR a hard time because at my wedding he failed to say, "You may kiss the bride" creating quite an awkward moment. Should I kiss her? Can I kiss her? Where's my cue? Twenty-five years later when renewing our vows he quickly made up for it, almost demanding that I kiss my bride. I did.

At a family gathering, never ask UR to say grace before a meal. He always claimed he was "off duty" and deferred to someone else.

Never share a hotel room with UR. He had a snore that would shake a house.

He was also dubbed as the "easiest faller asleeper." He could fall asleep in the middle of a conversation.

You probably didn't know this, but UR was a semiprofessional dart thrower. Well...at least during the annual Ciesielski Thanksgiving celebrations. Along with my dad, UR won the first ever Ciesielski dart tournament, and then quickly went into retirement as the reigning undefeated champion.

Years ago, we took a picture of UR playing Barbie's with my kids. He had a Barbie in one hand and a book on liturgy in the other. I don't know... maybe he didn't really know he was playing Barbie.

He loved to travel. He took many exotic trips to meet up with his traveling family, including Hong Kong, China, Dubai, Ireland, Mexico, Rome, and Germany. We recently learned his limit, though, when he sent his nephew Andy an email saying he would not be visiting him where he is stationed in Iraq. One thing that didn't surprise me was finding a huge box in his walk-in closet when we were clearing his things from the rectory. I opened it up and it was full of travel brochures, guide books, about every place and country that he'd been.

He loved his weekend getaways to visit his sister in Fort Wayne.

He loved spending time with his cousin Alice.

Words cannot express how proud his parents were the day of his ordination.

Difficult to do and last minute at times, he would often make special arrangements to cover Masses so he could be with his family.

We have video, the 8 mm reel-to-reel kind, of him "playing priest" as a young kid, long before he entered the seminary. He always knew what he was called to do with his life.

UR's dad, who we only called "King," built him an altar in an extra bedroom, and a large presider's chair for his young "pre-seminary practice sessions."

We were proud to be present as his family for the dedication of this church. What a proud accomplishment for all of you who worship here.

His love for his family was evident to us through you. Last week when we began planning and talking to people, everyone knew that UR was going to a family reunion this past weekend. Over the years we've met so many people who have said, "Oh, you're Ron's sister! How was his visit?" Or, "Oh, you're the police officer from Indianapolis!" Or, "Oh yeah, you're cousin Alice!" It seems he talked about us a little bit.

My sister loved going to the 4th of July fireworks in beautiful downtown Roanoke, Indiana, with UR. He enjoyed that.

We loved coming to the Pork and Corn Roast and the beautiful country setting here at St. Mary's.

As a teenager, he drove my sister from his home to a church function during a snowy day. During the drive his car did a 360 spin, luckily with no damage. But he begged my sister not to tell his dad... just a normal kid not wanting to get in trouble.

We searched frantically for documents containing UR's wishes for his funeral. Surely someone who is so focused on liturgy and its meaning would have hand-selected all of his readings, the Gospel and probably even the songs. We couldn't find anything and left it in the faithful and capable hands of all of the great presiders that will be here for the grand celebration. Then I got to thinking...what if in two weeks we find the document and it says he wanted his service in the small church with immediate family only?

Thank you to each and every one of you who had a special place in Ron's heart. You were more to him than a parishioner, or a coworker or a colleague or a friend....you were his family. Rest assured that you had as big of an impact on his life as he had had on yours.

We were proud to share UR with you. Thank you for sharing Fr. Ron with us.

We love ya, UR!

Fr. Robert Fedek

Vigil Presentation

With no doubt Fr. Ron Lewinski was one of the finest priests in the Archdiocese of Chicago. The list of his accomplishments is truly impressive. His contribution to the life of the Church, and the lives of those who had a chance to get to know him, cannot be measured. He had so much to offer to each one of us.

As I reflect on my relationship with Fr. Ron - three words come to my mind: a father, a friend and a mentor.

Fr. Ron was a holy and humble man who truly enjoyed sharing his life with others. His loving and generous heart enabled him to make a lot of friends. I was very lucky to be one of them. I had the privilege to meet Fr. Ron in the spring of 2005 when St. Mary's Annunciation Parish was selected for my deaconate pastoral experience. From the very moment I arrived at the doors of St. Mary's he welcomed me warmly and invited me to be part of his life. A few months later, right after my ordination, he traveled with me to Poland to join me and my family in celebrating my First Mass in my home parish. That journey was the beginning of what would become a wonderful working relationship and a valued friendship. During the following 12 years Fr. Ron accompanied me in every major step of my life. I can honestly say that he treated me like his son. He was a father to me.

Although he served as my mentor, we quickly became great friends. I was inspired by his generosity, by his humble and joyful acceptance of everyone into his life. He knew when to support me and when to challenge me. We learned so much from each other. We worked hard together; we shared the load of pastoral responsibilities. He shopped, I ironed. We cooked together, laughed together, and watched the news together at the end of the day. I taught him Polish vocabulary, he taught me English idioms. We walked the paths at Independence Grove, sharing the joys and burdens of serving a diverse and sometimes demanding community in a difficult and confusing world. We traveled together. He really enjoyed our last two trips to Poland during which we visited the birthplaces of his grandparents. He enjoyed meeting my family and I enjoyed meeting his. Many of you are here with us tonight - Ron's sister Diane and his brother-in-law Richard, his cousin Alice, his nephews Mark and Paul with his wife Dona; his nieces Cindy and Linda. We have many wonderful memories to cherish in our hearts from your numerous visits to our country-house here in Fremont Center. I will miss him a great deal, and I know that you will too.

Ron was an excellent mentor and teacher. In his ministry he was well known for his open-mindedness, creativity and thinking outside the box. He was not afraid to ask hard questions. He was a man with great vision of a strong and vibrant Church. He always encouraged people to grow, to stretch their minds, to search for new ways, to find more effective ways of ministering to God's people. He was an inspiration to many priests and many seminarians. He was a mentor and a friend to many of us. His death is a big loss to the Archdiocese of Chicago and to all of us. We will miss him dearly.

He introduced me to parish life and priesthood. I learned so much from him. We had many great conversations while sitting on our famous bench on the hill by the cemetery. I will miss those conversations. How good God has been to us!

My friends, as I look at all of you tonight, gathered here to remember and pray for one of the greatest men we have ever met in our lives, I am confident that Fr. Ron's life and his hard work will not be forgotten. His spirit will continue to dwell among us, especially here at St. Mary of the Annunciation - the parish that he loved so much and cared for with great dedication and passion. He had a dream, a desire to build a place, a community which would become the realization of everything he believed in and stood for. And he accomplished that dream. We are the beneficiaries of his generous heart and great mind.

We couldn't choose a better place than St. Mary's to celebrate his life. Farewell, Fr. Ron! Thank you for all you have done for us. You have made your mark on us. You have helped us to become better people and more faithful disciples. And thanks, Ron, for being a good father, a faithful friend, and a wonderful mentor. Please pray for us as you enjoy your retirement in heaven.

Deacon Howard Fischer

Vigil Presentation

Tonight we are gathered to celebrate the life of Ronald John Lewinski and to pray that the Lord will welcome his faithful servant into his heavenly kingdom. And we pray that the Lord will sustain us in our loss.

For the past week, I have felt a lot like Martha and Mary expressing their frustration to Jesus in the Gospel passage we just heard. You probably have felt likewise. How could something so wrenching, so unexpected, so seemingly unfair fit into the divine plan? And so we ask, "Lord, are you here with us or not?" But our path out of pain must be the same as Martha and Mary's: faith that Jesus is the resurrection who brings his faithful disciples to everlasting life. And Rev. Ronald J. Lewinski was nothing if not a faithful servant of Jesus Christ who lived with this conviction. And tonight amid our tears, we must sprinkle in a healthy dose of faith, hope and joy that Ron is now with the Lord whom he loved so much and served so well for 45 years of priestly ministry.

I can truly say that Ron Lewinski was my best friend. We talked almost every day. I relied heavily on his wisdom, guidance, vision, and companionship. I was a frequent recipient of his great generosity. I relished his wicked one-liners followed by that distinctive chuckle. Our relationship extends back over 30 years, which puts me firmly in the middle of the pack of his countless friends! It amazes me that a man who almost bragged about being a painful introvert had more close friends—and I mean friends, not just acquaintances—than dozens of us added together! Ron's relationships always had considerable substance, not just small talk. He had a profound impact on others. And somehow he kept in frequent touch with everyone!

As important as his friends were to him, his family was even more so. He loved the family holiday celebrations, get-togethers, and milestones. He told me several times how much he was looking forward to your gathering this past weekend. And I guess he still made his presence known on Saturday by the upside-down rainbow that appeared—as the food was being served, naturally! And while I may not have met everyone in the Lewinski-Ciesielski clan, I still know you well because of how often your family was a feature of my conversations with UR—Uncle Ron.

Fr. Robert, Fr. Andrew, and I have been discussing in recent days how much in our sorrow we are at a loss for words when it comes to talking about Ron and his profound influence in our lives. But we also observed that we could talk about him for hours on end and only scratch the surface of his life, talents, and ministry.

Fr. Ron was a modern renaissance man who possessed many talents and who always had more concurrent jobs and responsibilities than anybody I know. He was an author and a visionary who helped to shape not just the Church of Chicago but indeed the universal Church thanks to his passion and expertise for the Rite of Christian Initiation of Adults, which he helped create. His affection for this topic even as a seminarian earned him the nickname of "Ron the Baptist."

As head of the Office of Divine Worship, Ron was always proud that he organized the first-ever celebration of an RCIA rite by a pope when John Paul II celebrated mass in Grant Park in 1979. Over the decades he would literally travel around the world giving RCIA presentations to bishops and catechists alike.

Traveling to foreign lands, leading countless pilgrimages, and experiencing different people and cultures provided some unexpected lessons along the way. Once, when giving a talk in Australia, Ron spoke of the necessity for disciples to be rooted in Christ and the Gospel. After a while, he noticed that every time he used the word "rooted" his audience would smirk and chuckle. The bishop then explained to Ron that being "rooted" has sexual connotations in Australian English. Ooops!

Fr. Ron also greatly enjoyed being a parish priest, and being a teacher and mentor for young priests. He appreciated the opportunity to share the love of God with people in the real world and to be part of their highs and lows, both in daily life and in milestone moments like baptisms, weddings, and funerals. Of course, that could also lead to some interesting experiences.

Once when he was at St. Marceline's, I believe, Ron was in the sacristy with the groom before the start of a wedding. A large, rough biker sort of gentleman stormed into the room demanding that the groom repay an outstanding debt. Being the large, imposing physical presence that he was, Fr. Ron tried to intervene and act as the peacemaker, suggesting that this could be handled later as the wedding was about to start. "Look, priest, there ain't going to be no blanking wedding unless I get my blanking $500." When Ron tried to press for calm, the biker grabbed him, put him up against the wall, and slugged him, knocking him out cold. After Ron regained consciousness, he proceeded to celebrate the wedding.

Once after another wedding, one groomsman thanked Fr. Ron for his efforts and shoved three joints into his hand as tokens of gratitude. Ron was headed to visit someone in the hospital and didn't want to have three joints in his pocket, so when he got to his car he just threw them in the glove compartment. As he sped along, you guessed it, Ron gets pulled over by an officer of the law. The policeman asked Ron for his license and registration. As he opens the glove compartment, three joints roll out. Ron started blabbering an explanation that had to sound fantastical. The stunned officer just shook his head and said, "Father, I'm gonna pretend I didn't see that. Just get out of here, but watch your speed."

Of all the places he served, St. Mary of the Annunciation held a special place in his heart. With his special gift for envisioning and shaping the future, he nurtured this community through great growth from less than 500 families to 1600. The building in which we are gathered tonight has Ron's fingerprints all over it. This church, with its art and embedded spiritual symbolism, stands in testimony to his pastoral vision and love for the St. Mary community shown during his 18 years as pastor.

But his vision for St. Mary's and the Church wasn't focused on buildings and mortars. Over the years, he poured his boundless energy and talents into building a community of committed disciples, seeing parishes as (in his words) "greenhouses for growing saints."

Ron loved good food, and the restaurant business is going to take a big hit with his passing. While he definitely enjoyed fine dining, Ron could take in more mundane eateries as well, as my next story will show.

Last month, my wife and I took a trip to Italy with Ron. Each night at dinner, he always posed some question that involved reflection and personal sharing. One night he asked, "What was your most embarrassing meal experience?" After Maryann and I told our tales, he shared that he once took his friend and mentor Sr. Agnes Cunningham to a supposedly nice burger place for lunch... only to discover partway through the meal that this restaurant/bar was holding a lingerie show! (He's gonna zap me for telling this one!)

The stories could go on and on. I'm sure each of you has a few dozen you could readily add. It is important that we always and forever remember how fortunate and blessed we were to have the great gift of Rev. Ronald J. Lewinski in our lives. He was a tremendous force in the life of everyone here tonight and countless others beyond these walls. And that's why we all hurt so much right now. The impact he had on me and my family is beyond words. I miss him terribly.

But I think Fr. Ron would remind us tonight that we must not wallow in our grief, as tempting as that might be. His life and ministry were a testimony to the transcending love and mercy of God and to faith in the Resurrection of Jesus Christ. He sincerely tried his best to be an energetic disciple of the Lord and a faithful servant of his people. I can't help but think tonight of the words spoken at the funeral of Fr. Ron's good friend, Cardinal Bernardin: "Didn't he teach us? Didn't he show us the way?"

Yes, he did. So let us pray tonight that the Lord will welcome Ronald John Lewinski into heaven: "Well done, my good and faithful servant. Come, enter your Master's joy."

Thank you so much, my friend. Until we meet again...

Funeral Mass Homily

"Fellow Travelers on the Road to Emmaus"
St. Mary of the Annunciation – Mundelein, Illinois
Wednesday, July 26, 2017
By Fr. Andrew Liaugminas[6]

Sadness. Shock. Loss. These words, and many more, could well describe the emotions we're feeling today. Yet, even these words seem to pale in comparison with the weight of grief we're bearing. We're together, but grieving always feels so very personal. We're walking forward, but perhaps we only see a few feet ahead.

Emotions like these, which have become so close to us over these past few days, put us right in stride with the disciples on the road to Emmaus. Their world was utterly upside down. Jerusalem was supposed to be God's dwelling on earth, the "true pole of the earth" (Ps. 47:2), where the Messiah was expected to reign and to restore Israel. And yet, the One whom they believed to be Messiah and Redeemer came to Jerusalem, only to die. Unsure of everything else, they take to the road. And that's where we meet them today: on the way.

Ron would be the first to point out that there is something very ecclesial about this: being on the way with Christ. All of us have, in one way or another, walked with Ron along the way. Perhaps he walked with you as your brother, your uncle, your Shepherd, or as your dear friend. Perhaps he walked with you as your mentor, your colleague, or your fellow-traveler. How many times did our fellow traveler open the Scripture and break the Bread for us? How many times did our hearts burn within us as we walked with him along the Way? Let us listen again to the wisdom of our fellow-traveler.

Preaching on this passage, Ron once observed that the fundamental problem of the two disciples in today's Gospel was that

---

6. Fr. Liaugminas was ordained in 2010 and celebrated his First Mass of Thanksgiving at St. Mary of the Annunciation

they got "stuck on the death of Christ" and failed to comprehend that "the One walking with them is the One they seek...a living Person: the Person of Christ. Who is the way, the truth and the life". If they had recognized this, Ron added, they would have seen the prophesies being fulfilled in their very midst. Then their journey, rather than being a lifeless passage, would become a Paschal pilgrimage with the Savior. Rather than saying, "we had hoped that he would be the one to redeem us", as they said in today's Gospel, they would say, with Job in our First Reading, "I know that my Redeemer lives, and that he will at last stand forth upon the dust!"

Throughout his life, Ron lived out of the conviction that his Redeemer lives. If you were to ask him, Ron would tell you that he became a missionary of this message on March 3rd, 1946, the day of his Baptism at Assumption BVM Parish. There, in that holy corner of West Pullman, Ron died to this world and was reborn in Christ. From that point on, he lived a truly ecclesial existence that sprung from the waters of his Baptism. The "love and vibrancy" he experienced in his parish "sparked something inside [of him] that attracted [him] to the priesthood", and during his seminary studies, his heart was "burning within him" as he studied the writings of the Church Fathers on the liturgy and learned about the practices of the early Church.

In fact, so often did Ron share his zeal for the sacrament of Baptism that his classmates jokingly called him, "Ron the Baptist"! In this, they presaged Ron's future ministry and work on the RCIA; writing book on the Rite that are still used in parishes from Chicago to Singapore, and teaching it to many, including Pope St. John Paul II when he came to Chicago—the first time a Pope has celebrated the RCIA in the modern era. One of Ron's core insights on Baptism was that "with every Baptism, there's an anointing; and with every anointing, a missionary is born". This revolutionizes the way many look at Baptism. "I sometimes think", Ron would say, "that instead of issuing baptismal certificates on the day of Christening, we ought to be issuing job descriptions for anointed disciples!"

While Ron would take this message to all corners of the world—from Alaska to Germany, from UAE to Japan, Malaysia, and beyond—his conviction was always personal and local. If baptism makes us "anointed disciples" with a missionary calling, then we should not think of our parishes as having a mission, but 'the mission as having a Parish'. And what passion he had for forming disciples in the Parish context, for sharing people's lives, and for mentoring future Priests to do the same.

This is the Ron I came to know when—as a First-Year seminarian at Mundelein Seminary—I was assigned to him as my teaching Pastor and to St. Mary's for my First Year Field Ed. As Ron invited me to work with him on initiatives both in the Parish and beyond, I witnessed firsthand how he fostered mature Christian discipleship, and how truly "the mission has a Parish" here. Quickly, I came to see my time here not as a Field Ed requirement, but as a training ground to learn from a master. Ron rapidly became a close mentor, and this parish community, a home; and with this, I invited Ron to vest me as a Priest at my Ordination. It was under Ron's tutelage here that I celebrated my first Baptism the day after my Diaconate Ordination, and my First Mass the day after my Priestly Ordination. I owe an eternal debt of gratitude to Ron for these, and all the other ways that he has ignited my heart about the gift of the Priesthood and for his friendship.

While together we dug ditches and climbed glaciers, preparing this homily, my thoughts kept on going back to the memories of our common celebrations of the Triduum. Ron so loved the Triduum and unpacked its riches for us to appreciate as well. Concerned that young people were losing touch with the meaning of sacramental language and the beauty of the Triduum, one time Ron had the idea of holding a "Triduum Pep. Rally" here at St. Mary's! Maybe some of you were even there for it. Well, it was not just the kids who were getting into it, the Pep Rally reignited the adults' appreciation for the Triduum as well!

One of the warmest memories I have of the Triduum liturgy itself with Ron is the celebration of our Lord's Last Supper and the Priesthood. Standing just feet from the baptismal font Ron designed to call to mind tomb and womb, at the start of Mass, Ron would always revel in singing the Holy Thursday entrance antiphon: "We should glory in the Cross of our Lord Jesus Christ, in whom is our salvation, life and resurrection, through whom we are saved and delivered" (Gal. 6:14). For Ron, the antiphon was an anthem.

Literally, the sung version of this antiphon used in countless Parishes across the world was composed by Steven Janco in honor of Ron Lewinski: "We should glory in the Cross…"

This love of the Paschal Mystery flows out of a baptismal spirituality, echoed in our Second Reading today: "Are you unaware that we who were baptized into Christ Jesus were baptized into his death?" St. Paul does not relent on his conviction: "We know that Christ, raised from the dead, dies no more; death no longer has power over him", and thus, having died with Christ at Baptism, "we believe that we shall also live with him". And how right it is to glory in this fact.

With this, let's return for one last time to the disciples on the road to Emmaus and to Ron's insight that the fundamental problem of these two disciples was that they failed to comprehend that "the One Who is walking with them is the One they seek…a living Person: the Person of Christ". The disciples were hoping that Christ would enter into his glory, indeed. But since suffering and death had no place in their vision, their hope died on Calvary. So erroneous was their vision of sharing in Christ's glory that when the glorified Christ himself does appear to them, they mistake him for a Stranger. The Lord gently re-orients their understanding starting with one simple, yet direct question: "Was it not necessary that the Christ should suffer all these things and so enter into his glory?" (Lk. 24:26). And precisely because of who he is, his sufferings and his glory open up to include everyone incorporated into his Body, the Church. And all those "anointed" in the Anointed One, from the waters of Baptism on, share in Christ's suffering with the hope that they might share in his Resurrection. Hence, living our baptismal calling includes totality of one's life, one's gifts, one's joys and one's sufferings—as Gaudium et Spes states at the outset—and doing this precisely through the Church: through liturgical praise, through the fulfillment of one's vocation, through works of mercy and evangelization.

This liturgical, scriptural, sacramental, and deeply pastoral vision of the Church was at the core of Ron's pastoral life, homilies, and writings. And he lived it out in many roles throughout his lifetime: as Director of the Office for Divine Worship in the Archdiocese of Chicago, in speaking engagements in far-off places like Australia,

South Africa, Singapore and Malaysia, as a Pastor who helped refound St. Mary of the Annunciation into a community of 1,800+ households. His parish experiences fed his imagination and led to new ideas that evolved into workshops, lectures, articles and creating new pastoral models. Closely observing Catholic education him led to help found the first Archdiocesan Catholic Middle School, Frassati Catholic Academy. His pastoral and administrative experiences led to his work with Parish Transformation, and more recently, Renew My Church and the Office of Parish Vitality and Mission. This involvement gave him the opportunity to help others with lessons he learned, but which he knew he would never have enough time to implement. Your presence here is a testament to the width and breadth of his ministry and God's work through him.

So, how does one sum this all up? The last time I saw Ron in person was in Rome. I was finishing my doctoral studies and he came over for a pilgrimage with Deacon Howard Fischer and his wife, Marianne. We arranged to celebrate Mass together in the crypt of St. Peter's Basilica, just steps from the tomb of the Apostle. Ron presided at Mass, and in his homily, preached about the importance of faith: faith that carries us through the difficult times of life. At the end of Mass, we processed back to the Sacristy of St. Peter's to devest. Now, you have to have your espresso before going to St. Peter's because you really never know you you're going to meet. Sure enough, as Ron and I were devesting in the Sacristy there, I looked to my left and saw a distinguished gentleman staring at me. Fortunately, I did have my espresso earlier that morning, and so I recalled that this gentleman on my left was the Vatican Monsignor who oversaw the liturgies for Cardinal Cupich's Consistory events in Rome. After saying hello, I wanted to introduce him to Ron, a fellow lover of the liturgy. But as I started the introduction, I quickly realized how incapable I was of summarizing Ron's role: "Monsignor, here's Fr. Ron Lewinski, Co-Director of the Department of Parish Vitality and Mission of the Archdiocese of Chicago."

But as I was attempting to communicate this, I felt that my words were communicating only a fraction of what Ron does and stands for. Ron must have sensed this. Afterwards he told me, "Andrew, what I usually say in these situations is that I'm a servant of the Cardinal and of the Church".

Let's let that self-chosen title, which animated his ministry for 45 years, remain as Ron's epitaph. The Gospel concludes with Christ revealing his glory in the reading of Scripture and the Breaking of the Bread (Lk. 24:25-35). As we gather today to do the same sacramental actions, remembering the sacrifice of Christ that conquered death and opened for us the light of glory, let us pray for the soul of our dear brother, Ron. Each of us has stories about how he walked with us and showed us Christ's presence in our pilgrimage of life. May Christ's presence among us today in Word and Sacrament heal our sorrow and strengthen our hope. In prayer, let us accompany our brother Ron as he makes his final procession down this aisle, passed the font to the grave, in his continued pilgrimage to the Father. Let us pray that this servant may now take his seat at the Father's Table, hearing the Master at last say to him, "Well done, good and faithful servant…enter into your Master's joy" (Mt. 25:23)—a verse that Ron used to love to quote.

And as Ron told me before I celebrated my first Funeral Liturgy, "Ultimately, you don't need to say too much in a funeral homily, the Funeral Liturgy says it all." Listen to the words of this liturgy. Listen to the hope, the promise. Come to Christ and let us commend our brother, Ron, to the Lord.

Tributes

John Gannon

Author of Sesquicentennial Parish history Nothing is Impossible with God
Former parishioner at St. Mary of the Annunciation

From 2013 to 2020, John was a parishioner at St. Mary of the Annunciation. In 2013-2014, he was co-chair of the Sesquicentennial History Committee and worked closely with Fr. Ron while writing a parish history. His remembrance, below, was originally published shortly after Fr. Ron's funeral.

Fr. Ron Lewinski, our beloved former pastor and a dear friend of many in the parish community, passed away unexpectedly on July 19, 2017. In his nearly eighteen years as pastor of St. Mary, Fr. Ron, in essence, re-founded the parish, leading the construction of our beautiful church, founding Frassati Catholic Academy, and presiding over the growth of the parish from a rural community of fewer than 600 families to the thriving suburban parish of over 1600 families that St. Mary's is today. His passing has left an enormous void in the lives of his many friends and relatives and in the life of the wider Church in the Archdiocese of Chicago.

The breadth of Fr. Ron's influence and the depth of the love and admiration that so many have for him was reflected in his magnificent funeral liturgy, celebrated at St. Mary's on July 26th and attended by over a thousand people. Cardinal Blasé Cupich presided at the emotional and triumphal liturgy that was con-celebrated by eight bishops and 127 priests. In his homily, Fr. Andrew Liaugminas, one of the many young priests and seminarians whom Fr. Ron mentored, spoke of his friend's love for the sacrament of Baptism, his world-renowned expertise on the Rite of Christian Initiation of Adults, and his reverence for the liturgy and especially for the Eucharist as the source and summit of Christian life.

At a prayer service, held the night before the funeral, Fr. Ron's close friends Deacon Howard Fischer and Fr. Robert Fedek, as well as his nephew Paul Ciesielski, recalled Fr. Ron as a loyal friend, a man of humility and a quick and dry sense of humor, a persistent and patient mentor and a devoted uncle known affectionately to his many nieces, nephews and great-nieces and nephews as simply UR. Hundreds of people attended the visitation in the hours leading up to the prayer service, exchanging condolences and telling stories about Fr. Ron.

Fr. Ron Lewinski was indeed many things. For 45 years he was a good and devoted priest and a visionary of towering intellect whose influence on the Church in the Archdiocese of Chicago and beyond is immeasurable. More than that though, he was a beloved brother, uncle and cousin and a loyal and true friend who made a profound and lasting impact on countless lives. And for almost eighteen years, he was our good shepherd whose legacy lives on in the beautiful church he built, the prayerful and reverent liturgy he fostered, and the vibrant and welcoming community of faith he nurtured here in Fremont Center. Fr. Ron's love for this parish community is evident in the fact that it was his wish to be buried here in our parish cemetery.

In the coming months and years, the parish and Frassati Catholic Academy will find other ways to honor Fr. Ron, and the entire community of St. Mary's can carry on his legacy by continually striving to be missionary disciples, by continuing to celebrate the Eucharist with prayerful reverence, and by encouraging vocations to the priesthood and religious life from among the youth of the community. May perpetual light shine upon Fr. Ronald J. Lewinski and may his soul and the souls of all the faithful departed, through the mercy of God, rest in Peace.

~ ~ ~

Fr. Paul Turner

"Fr. Ron: A Leader in Initiation"
Pastoral Liturgy 48:5 (September | October 2017):20

The Rite of Christian Initiation of Adults bookended my long friendship with Fr. Ron Lewinski. I started meeting people associated with the North American Forum on the Catechumenate while helping organize an institute in Kansas City in 1989. Several of them told me about Ron and spoke glowingly of his qualities. He was a scholar with a pastoral heart. An effective presenter. A good team worker. I had been ordained only ten years.

"Do you know him?"

"No."

"You could become like him," his colleagues said.

Friendship was instant when Ron and I first worked together on a Forum institute. Indeed, it was easy to see in him a role model for priestly ministry. With a pastor's heart and parish experience, he served the parochial, diocesan, national and international Church, making many disciples, many friends.

In 1993 we both ended up at the Intercontinental Symposium on Catechumenal Theology in Lyon, France, which included presenters from the United States such as the mild-mannered Catherine Dooley and the thundering James Dunning. Afterward, Ron and I took some time to explore the French countryside, share thoughts about liturgical theology, relax, read, laugh and eat.

Ron's Guide for Sponsors (Liturgy Training Publications, aka LTP), is the book for which Ron is probably best known. Many Catholics feel daunted by the idea of serving as a sponsor for a catechumen, but Ron's book has instilled confidence and excitement in the hearts of those now sharing their faith. The book exemplified Ron's "You-can-do-this" attitude that characterized much of his work as a parish priest.

Less known was the work Ron did behind the scenes for the American edition of the Rite of Christian Initiation of Adults, published in 1988. He served on a small task force that helped develop the adapted rites for candidates who already enjoyed a valid baptism. He worked on developing such ceremonies as the Rite of Welcoming, the Rite of Sending, the Call to Continuing Conversion, and the Penitential Rite for candidates. These appear only in the American edition, but they have been widely copied throughout the English-speaking world.

In recent years, my work led me to criticize these rites, and Ron took it all in stride. He began to rethink some of his earlier assumptions about baptized candidates, and I gained new appreciation into the pastoral efforts made in the late 1980s to enflesh the RCIA with the complex American societal milieu.

The two of us gave major presentations at the annual meeting of the Federation of Diocesan Liturgical Commissions in 2014. The FDLC had helped recruit the Center for Applied Research in the Apostolate to survey the implementation of the national statutes on the RCIA. Ron and I each delivered papers on the results. As expected, his remains a masterful analysis of contemporary parish initiation practice.

Most recently, LTP issued Ron's last book, "An Introduction to the RCIA." In his typical easy-to-read style of writing, Ron offers encouragement to those just becoming acquainted with the mission of escorting people through catechesis and toward the sacraments of initiation. The book fills a need. The turnover of people leading RCIA ministry in parishes remains heavy, and some priests sheepishly admit that they received little formation on the complex rites of initiation in their seminary formation. Ron's book patiently, respectfully and clearly explains the process of initiation.

LTP gave me the honor of writing an endorsement for Ron's book, which appears on the back cover: "Ron Lewinski has more experience with the Rite of Christian Initiation of Adults than almost any other person on earth. He will bring you intense knowledge, practical guidance, gentle challenges, and increased confidence. If you want a basic knowledge of Christian initiation, and if you have not yet met this author, you owe it to yourself to read this book."

The book came into my hands in July 2017. Ten days later I received word that Fr. Ron Lewinski had died.

Since first hearing about Ron through the Forum, I had come to know him, but I could never become like him.

Like many others, I am grateful to the North American Forum on the Catechumenate and Liturgy Training Publications for making Ron's work available. We have all sharpened our insights on initiation because of his patient work, clear explanations, challenging ideas, and faithful devotion. He has made us better professionals and persons. We join in prayer now to thank God for the gift that Ron has been to us, and to ask God to welcome him into the heart of the paschal mystery that Ron so lovingly explored through the Rite of Christian Initiation of Adults.

Concordance

68's generation: Elst
ACTA: Dowling, Eipers, Senior
Advent for Women: Thompson
Affirmation: Eipers, Turner
Africa: Eipers, Karecki, Lyman
Altar boy: Zygmunt
Anniversary: Fahey, Hertel, Klugiewicz, Tonelli, J Wojcik
Art and Environment in Catholic Worship; Williamson
Australia: Berchmans, Fedek
Austria: Zucco
Author: Barrett, Cunningham, Fisher, Lyman, Poletto, Tufano,
Baptism: Barrett, Bujan, Cunningham, Canary, Cunningham, Hertel, Lucas, Matijevic, Matousek, Raab, Stowe, Tufano, Williamson, J Wojcik
Baptismal font: Barrett, Elst, Hendricks, Hertel, Karecki, Zagula
Belize: Hertel, Kuderna
Bench: Elst, Fedek
Bible: Cunningham, Tonelli
Boycott: Tonelli
Buddhism: Matijevic
Built of Living Stones (BLS): Barrett, Kicanas, Williamson
Candidate: Barrett
Canon Law: Bailey, Tonelli
Cardinal Bernardin: Bailey, Elst, Fedek, Kicanas, Markiewicz, Poletto, P Wojcik
Cardinal Cody: Pollard, Tufano, Williamson
Cardinal Cupich: Canary, Elst, Cunningham, Lyman, Matijevic, Williamson
Cardinal George: Berchmans, Canary, Cunningham, Elst, Lohan, Lyman, Matijevic, Williamson, P Wojcik
Catechesis: Eipers
Catechumen: Barrett, Elst, Karecki, Matijevic, Raab, Tufano, Turner, Williamson
CCD: see Office of Divine Worship
Change: Bailey, Barrett, Canary, Eipers, Elst, Fahey, Fisher, Gorman, Kartje, Kicanas, Lucas, Markiewicz, Matijevic, Raab, Riggio, Robinson, Tonelli, Turner, Williamson, J Wojcik, P Wojcik, Zygmunt
Chaplain: Fahey, Tonelli
Chaplain of the U.S. Congress: Fahey
Chicago Blackhawks: Arata
Chicago Catechumenate Magazine: Gensler
Christian: Barrett, Dowling, Matijevic, Tonelli, Williamson, Zygmunt
Church (as a building): Canary, Cunningham, Elst, Hendricks, Lucas, Markiewicz, Turner, Zagula
Church (as people): Canary, Cunningham, Elst, Fahey: Hendricks, Markiewicz, Turner, Zagula
Church Fathers: Cunningham, Kartje, Pollard
Confirmation: Barrett, Stowe, Tonelli
Contextual Architecture: Lohan
Convert: Bailey, Robinson, Tonelli
Curia: Markiewicz
Dialogue: Elst, Gorman
Diantha Hall: Gensler
Discipleship: Barrett, Cupich, Hertel
Docent: Hendricks, Zagula
Easter: Barrett, Canary, Fahey, Matijevic, Matousek, Poletto, Robinson, Zygmunt
Ecclesiology: Canary, Cunningham

Ecumenical: Tonelli
Emmaus Drive: Hendricks
Epiphanies: Barrett, Karecki
Eucharist: Bailey, Barrett, Elst, Cunningham, Hertel, Lohan, Lyman, Markiewicz, Matijevic, Matousek, Pollard, Robinson, Tonelli, Turner, Walsh
Eucharistic Chapel: Elst, Lohan, Lyman, Pollard, Tonelli
Evangelize: Matijevic, Tonelli, P Wojcik
Expansion (project): Canary, Cunningham, Elst, Kicanas, Lyman, Riggio, Washburn, Zagula
Family: Arata, Bujan, Canary, Fahey, Hertel, Lyman, Markiewicz, Matijevic, Matousek, Stowe, Thompson, J Wojcik, Zucco
Farnsworth House: Lohan
First Eucharist (Communion): Barrett, Hertel, Matijevic, Stowe
Formation: Barrett, Cupich, Eipers, Gensler, Kartje, Lyman, Markiewicz
France: Cunningham, Fahey, Tufano, Turner
Frassati Academy: Canary, Lyman, Turner
Fundraising: Barrett, Gensler, Turner
Funeral: D Ciesielski, Eipers, Elst, Hertel, Lyman, Matijevic, Pollard, J Wojcik, Zygmunt
Germany: Bailey, Elst, Fahey, Lohan, Pollard, Senior, Tufano
Gethsemani: Fahey, Hertel, Kicanas, Thompson, Tonelli
Gifts: Barrett, Bujan, Canary, Cunningham, Dowling, Eipers, Elst, Gensler, Hertel, Lucas, Lyman, Markiewicz, Matijevic, Matousek, Pollard, Raab, Thompson, Turner, P Wojcik, Zagula
Glory in the Cross: Janco
Golf: Fahey, Zucco
Good shepherd: Hertel
Grant: Dowling, Senior
Greece: Elst
Healing Mass: Bujan
History: Barrett, Canary, Dowling, Elst, Karecki, Riggio, Tonelli, Williamson, Zagula, Zucco
Holy Land: Bujan, Fischer, Matousek, P Wojcik
Holy Name Cathedral: Bailey, Canary, Elst, Matijevic, Tonelli
Holy Spirit: Barrett, Hertel, Hendricks
Home-schooling: Payette
Homily: Arata, Bailey, Berchmans, Elst, Hertel, Korecki, Lyman, Payette, Thompson, Tonelli, Washburn, Zagula
Immersion: see Baptismal font
Indonesia: Zygmunt
Islamic: Zygmunt
Italy: Fahey, Hertel, Lyman, Zucco
Jewish: Tonelli
Kansas: Gensler
Kelly, Mathew: Lucas
Keusal, Gene: Bailey, Markiewicz, Matousek, Poletto
Latin: Canary, Cunningham, Tonelli, Tufano
Lecture: Fedek, Karecki, Tonelli
Lent: Elst, Fahey, Hertel, Lyman, Matijevic,
Liturgical consultant: Williamson
Liturgical: Barrett, Canary, Elst, Gregory, Huck, Karecki, Lohan, Poletto, Scavone, Tonelli, Turner, Williamson, T Wojcik, Zygmunt
Liturgy Conference: Williamson

Liturgy of the Hours: Canary, Walsh
Liturgy Training Publications (LTP): Barrett, Broccolo, Huck, Tufano, Williamson
Liturgy: Barrett, Eipers, Elst, Fahey, Fedek, Fischer, Gensler, Hendricks, Hertel, Karecki, Kartje, Matijevic, Riggio, Tonelli, Walsh, Washburn, P Wojcik
Loyola University: Fahey, Markiewicz, Matijevic, Zygmunt
Malaysia: Berchmans, Fedek
Mandela, Nelson: Karecki
Marquette University: Berchmans
Men (Fellowship) of St. Joseph: Kuderna, Lyman, Robinson, Zagula
Mentor: Berchmans, Bujan, Eipers, Janco, Matijevic, Matousek, Pollard, Scavone, Thompson, Turner, Walsh
Merton, Thomas: Fahey, Kicanas, Thompson, Tonelli, P Wojcik
Meyer Center: Matijevic
Ministry: Arata, Broccolo. Cupich, Dowling, Eipers, Elst, Fedek, Fischer, Gensler, Gregory, Kicanas, Markiewicz, Matijevic, Pollard, Powell, Turner, Williamson
Mission: Canary, Eipers, Elst, Fedek, Gensler, Gorman, Hertel, Kuderna, Lyman, Matijevic, Raab, Raab, Williamson
Mission statement: Gensler
Mundelein Seminary: Broccolo, Cunningham, Elst, Fedek, Gorman, Hertel, Matijevic, Pollard, Tonelli, J Wojcik
Music: Riggio, Scavone, Tonelli, Williamson
Narthex: Behm, Cunningham, Elst, Klugiewicz, Lohan, Pollard
North American Forum: Raab, Tufano, Turner
Notre Dame University: Raab
Office for Divine Worship (ODW): Broccolo, D Ciesielski, Eipers, Elst, Huck, Lucas, Markiewicz, Raab, Tufano, Turner, Williamson
Office of Mission and Vitality: Fedek, Matijevic
Organ: Fisher, Lohan, Markiewicz, Scavone, Tonelli, J Wojcik, Zygmunt
PADS: Barrett, Poletto
Parish (Pastoral) Council: Lyman, Matousek, Pollard, Powell, Thompson, Washburn, Zygmunt
Parish Transformation: Fedek, Matijevic, Matousek, Pollard, Williamson
Patrology/Patristics: Canary, Cunningham, Tonelli
Pilgrimage: Bujan, Hertel, Matijevic, Matousek, Robinson
Poland: Fahey, Fedek
Pope: Fischer, Karecki, Tonelli, Tufano, Williamson, P Wojcik
Pork and Corn Roast: Lyman, Washburn, Zagula
Protestant: Bailey, Robinson, Tonelli, Zygmunt
Pullman: D Ciesielski, Klugiewicz
Quigley Preparatory: D Ciesielski, Matijevic
RCIA: Bailey, Barrett, Canary, Cunningham, Elst, Fedek, Fischer, Gensler, Hertel, Huck, Karecki, Klugiewicz, Lyman, Poletto, Raab, Thompson, Tonelli, Tufano, Turner, Williamson, J Wojcik, P Wojcik, Zagula
Reflection: Bujan, Cupich, Elst, Kuderna, Lucas, Turner
Religious Education Program (REP): Hendricks, Matousek, Tufano
Renew My Church: Bailey, Fedek, Lucas, Matijevic, Senior, Williamson, J Wojcik, P Wojcik
Renewal: Bailey, Broccolo, Cupich, Elst, Huck, Pollard, Turner, Williamson, J Wojcik, P Wojcik
Rescue: Zagula
Retirement: Cupich, Fedek
Retreat: Fahey, Fedek, Gensler, Hertel, Lucas, Payette, Raab, Thompson, Tonelli
Role model: Elst, Turner

Roman Canon: Matijevic
Roman Rite: Pollard
Rome: Elst, Karecki, Markiewicz, Tonelli, P Wojcik
Russian Orthodox church: Zygmunt
Sabbatical: Bailey, Hertel, Kicanas, Williamson, P Wojcik
Sacramental theology: Canary, Karecki
Sacraments: Barrett, Bujan, Canary, Hertel, Kartje, Matijevic, Matousek, Stowe, Turner, Zucco
Sacrosanctum Concilium: Barrett, Canary, Pollard
Sanctuary: Elst, Hendricks
Saudi Arabia: Poletto
School Board: Pollard, Thompson
Scripture: Barrett, Bujan, Cunningham, Gorman, Matousek, Payette, Pollard, Tonelli, Zagula
Second Vatican Council see Vatican II
Seminarian: Cunningham, Gorman, Kartje, Matijevic, Pollard, J Wojcik
Serenity: Washburn
Servant leadership: Bujan
Shepherd: Elst, Hertel, Hendricks, Matousek, Williamson
Spirituality: Cunningham, Elst, Fedek, Lohan, Thompson, Tonelli, J Wojcik
Sponsor: Bailey, Barrett
SPRED: Stowe
St. Frances of Rome parish: Canary, Fahey, Walsh, J Wojcik, Zygmunt
St. Thomas Acquinas: P Wojcik
Stations of the Cross: Hendricks, Zagula
Steeple: Behm, Hendricks, Zagula
Swimming: Fahey, J Wojcik. Zagula
Switzerland: Fahey
Tabernacle: Gensler, Kartje, Tonelli
Tapestry: Barrett, D Ciesielski, Karecki
Thailand: Bailey
The Pivotal Pastor: Kartje
Theology: Canary, Cunningham, Elst, Fischer, Gorman, Karecki, Markiewicz, Matijevic, Tonelli
Town Hall: Barrett, Hertel, Markiewicz, Matousek, Zagula
Training: Hendricks, Lucas, Pollard
Triduum: Barrett, Hertel, Janco, Kartje, Lyman
United Arab Emirates: Eipers
University of St. Mary of the Lake: see Mundelein Seminary
USCCB: Barrett, Kicanas
Vatican II: Barrett, Berchmans, Broccolo, Canary, Elst, Fahey, Gensler, Gorman, Hertel, Huck, Kartje, Kicanas, Klugiewicz, Lohan, Lucas, Matijevic, Pollard, Raab, Senior, Tonelli, Turner, Walsh, Williamson, J Wojcik, P Wojcik, Zygmunt
Vigil candles: Barrett, Hertel
Washing feet: Hertel, Lyman, Matousek
Windows: Hendricks, Zagula
Wirtz, Bill: Arata
Wisdom: Barrett, Downing, Eipers, Janco
Woodstock generation: Elst
Workshop: Eipers, Janco, Karecki, Klugiewicz, Tufano
Zulu: Karecki

ABOUT THE EDITOR

djkennebeck@emmaus-way.com

David J. Kennebeck is author of **The Pivotal Pastor** (ISBN 979-8-9866668-0-8 www.emmaus-way.com/tpp), a story about Fr. Ron Lewinski's first six-year term as pastor at St. Mary of the Annunciation. During that time (1996-2002), the parish built a new church that can seat four times more than the old one; the number of ministries increased from half a dozen to over two dozen; and the number of parish households doubled.

Mr. Kennebeck was a parishioner at St. Mary of the Annunciation parish from 1983 until 2015. He has an undergraduate degree from Western Illinois University, and a Certificate in Pastoral Leadership from a Masters in Leadership Studies at Lewis University in Romeoville, Illinois. While at St. Mary of the Annunciation, he served on the Pastoral Council, the PR and Communications Committee, and various ministries. He created the parish's first website in 1998.

He and his wife are retired and enjoy visiting with family and friends. He welcomes comments, questions, and especially corrections.

Visit www.emmaus-way.com/tpp to learn about the companion volume "The Pivotal Pastor" and to access another photo gallery.